Essentials of Ramadan, the Fasting Month

قال رسول الله (ص) فيمايـروه عن ربه : فال
الله عز وجل:
« كلُّ عمل ابن آدم له إلا الصيام فـإنه لي وأنا
أجــــزي بـه ••• » رواه مسلم

The Messenger of Allah (saas)
reported in a hadith Al-Qudsi that Allah (SWT) said:

"All services of the son of Adam are for him except fasting.
It is for Me, and I will reward him for it.''

(Bukhari/Muslim)

ESSENTIALS OF
RAMADAN,
THE FASTING MONTH

By
Tajuddin Bin Shu'aib

Islamic Book Center, Inc.
Los Angeles, California, USA

Essentials of Ramadan, The Fasting Month

Copyright © 1991 by Tajuddin B. Shu'aib
Published by:
  Islamic Book Center, Inc.
  P.O. Box 43554, Los Angeles, California 90043

Library of Congress Catalog Card Number: 91-071809
Tajuddin B. Shu'aib
  Essentials of Ramadan, the Fasting Month
ISBN 09610618-1-2

Manufactured and bound in the United States of America.

ABOUT THE AUTHOR

SHEIKH TAJUDDIN B. SHU'AIB was born in Accra, Republic of Ghana, West Africa. He received his Islamic education at Islamic University Median, Saudi Arabia. While in England in 1976 he joined the Muslim Educational Trust in London and was put in charge of the Islamic studies program in the City of Luton. He came to the United States of America in 1977 and worked with the World Community of Islam in the West at the organizations west coast headquarters. In 1981 he was co-founder of Masjid As-Salaam and Islamic Studies Center, where he is working now as the director and Imam. Sheikh Shu'aib is an Islamic educator and has travelled to several states to deliver lectures in masajid and universities. He has also made several radio and television appearances and has been interviewed by *Time* magazine. He is the author of the now famous book *The Prescribed Prayer Made Simple.*

CONTENTS

ACKNOWLEDGMENT

THIS BOOK is dedicated to Allah Subhanahu wa Ta'ala whose guidance, help and grace were instrumental in making this humble work a reality. I have many people to thank for their assistance.

Sister Linda El-Amin processed the manuscript. Sister Muslimah and Muhammad Alaby and Dr. Ismail Abdul Karim provided fresh perspectives and fine editorial counsel. I am indebted to brother Ibrahim M. Al Habr, director of Masjid Ibn Taymiyyah, Los Angeles California and Imam Ghurmallah A. Al-Ghamdi, Imam Masjid Riverside, California for their technical and scholastic inputs. My sincere thanks to Islamic Affairs Department, Embassy of the Custodian of the Two Holy Masajid, especially Prince Muhammad bin Faisal and his deputy Khalil Al-Khalil for the inestimable support for this book. I want to express my appreciation to every person who contributed with either inspirational or actual work with this book. I pray to Allah that He rewards each a beatify reward.

PREFACE

All praise is due to Almighty Allah, the Lord of the universe, may His peace and the blessing descend upon the most noble of all the Prophets and the Messengers, Muhammad bin Abdullah (saas), his entire family and the companions.

Examining the Islamic library of English language, one is shocked to realize the scarcity of books in virtually all subjects of Islam including, creed (tawheed), history, Arabic language, Fiqh (practical applications), as well as general tenants. Besides, what one finds in circulation is replete with errors and some outright distortion in the translation of certain text of Al-Qur'an and the Hadith while others are loosely prepared, Islamic detached, generalized and uninformed. The reason for this dilemma is the scarcity of sound Islamic knowledge and the lack of competent scholars specializing in the sciences and letters of Islam who believe in the methodology of earlier generations of Muslim scholars and who enjoy the widespread acceptance among the Muslims because of their depth of knowledge of Islam, sincere conviction of its original orientation and their noble and impeccable conduct.

Therefore, I implore all concerned Muslims and students of Islam who have earned the respect of Muslims because of their drawing on experience and examples of the early generations to promptly embark on the mission of impacting the truth about Islam with teaching, propagation, and writing. They must write in English in the subjects that have not been written on, or complement in writing what needs to be complemented and focus on correcting what stands in need of correction.

I urge also the generous benevolent Muslims, individuals and organizations to assist the Islamic workers and writers to produce and publicize their writings.

We at Islamic Foundation of Sheikhul Islam bin Taymiyah are sparked by our dissatisfaction of both what is or is not available in the arena of Islamic literature by supporting these worthy and noble causes for that is in accordance with the statement of the Almighty Allah: "...Help ye one another in righteousness and piety..." (Al-Qur'an, 4:2). We, therefore, decided to assist in publishing this book "Essentials of Ramadan, the Fasting Month" by Tajuddin B. Shu'aib. The book is committed to clarification of many issues central to the Islamic by-laws on fasting and to which every Muslim needs to know as it treats this important pillar of Islamic religion and the honoring of the blessed month of Ramadan. It is our belief that this book is unique in its kind and a resource in the Islamic English library. We pray that it will be a valuable addition in the Islamic literature and most helpful in observing what Allah ordained on us in fasting, Alms giving, and nightly prayers. We hopefully ask Allah to accept this effort from us all and make it worthwhile.

Ibrahim bin Muhammad Al-Habr
Director Masjid Ibn Taymiyah

INTRODUCTION

All praise are due to Allah, Subhanahu wa Ta'ala, the Sustainer of the worlds. I pray that His peace and blessings descend upon the Most Noble of all the Messengers of Allah, Muhammad Bin Abdullah, *sallallahu 'Alaihi wa salam*, his family and companions.

Whenever the earth turns and another month of Ramadan approaches, happiness and joy return to the Ummah, for with it comes two of the greatest gifts of Allah, namely the fasting month of Ramadan and the celebration of the revelation of Al Qur'an.

This is an in-depth resumé of the essential rules and laws on the fiqh of fasting, designed to provide the reader with an explanation for both the spiritual and physical significance and the uniqueness of this remarkable act of worship. We desire to clarify major points on fasting. Our focus is the relevance of this divine discipline on life and living as well as the interpretation of related texts on fasting based on Al-Quran and the Sunnah of the Messenger of Allah (saas). This book serves as a guide and reference for courses on Islamic studies.

Fasting is an eloquent expression of Allah, leading this Ummah to the gates of His mercy, a key to unlocking the mysteries of His nearness. While humanity is divided on the basic elements of the notion of the Creator, a Muslim is far ahead of the rest of the world in this field and travelling at the speed of light to the neighborhood of the Throne of the Creator. Where else would you find a discipline that provides direct communication between the servant and the Served? Where else would you have an act of *'Ebadah* that enriches self-worth, self-strength, self-rebuilding, self discipline and control? Where else would one find a discipline that moves the believer from the unauthentic to the authentic as does the institution of fasting? Where else would you find a discipline that enriches the vital needs of the human being, both physical and spiritual? Praise be to Allah!

The institution of fasting is a unique form of worship prescribed as part of the overall system of Islam. Its uniqueness mirrors the uniqueness of the human being, a creature of physical and spiritual parts whose excellence depends on the right proportion of these two parts. Too much of the physical material will

1

ruin man, and too much of the spiritual will, too. Fasting orients the observer to the art of balancing the spiritual essentials with physical needs, a vivid proof that there is in all of us will power, a pivotal element that controls our actions. This will be needed to help us curb the animalistic tendencies originating from the stomach, in full. It makes us forget about our beginning, it awakens the mind and rekindles clear thinking and consciousness of Allah. Fasting is the sobering of the mind and the reconstruction of our spiritual faculties.

Fasting has instilled in food and beverages a religious legitimacy, as its amount and the hour taken are expressed in terms of *deen* religion, and chewing and drinking at the prescribed intervals equal praise and glorification of Allah. It makes the individual ready and primed to meet the Creator. You see, it has never been easy trying to gain access to the nearness of Allah, SWT, due to several considerable obstacles obstructing our view, mainly ignorance, multiple images or double vision, passive will power, time, place, culture, upbringing, and prejudice. Fortunately, the gates that lead to the nearness of Allah swing both ways with the help of fasting.

Fasting cures the double vision that many people suffer in the realm of spirituality. The inauguration of Fasting eliminates the middleman, a spiritual broker, an insidious opinion held by some that a believer can only gain access to Allah through another, who is endowed with superpowers. No, indeed, Allah is ineffable yet approachable. It is the sum and scope of Allah's 'Ebadah that clarifies all the acts of 'Ebadah including Salaat. Fasting renders this magnificent and beautiful idea of Tawhid of Allah, there being no deity but Allah, and Muhammad being His Messenger, into an effective power charge, a potent and effective concept for focusing and organizing one's world view and epitomizing the religious and psychological orientation of the believer.

On the other hand, Ramadan was the host month for the inauguration of the final revelation, Al-Quran Al-Azeem. Allah (SWT) bestowed this book upon humanity through His Messenger, Muhammad bin Abdullah. The reading of Al-Quran has been mandated by its Author, Allah himself, for the believers all the time, but more so in the month of Ramadan, as this is reported from the Messenger. Muslims past and present have always mixed fasting with reading of Al-Quran. Perhaps the reason for this is that one of the objectives of Iblis (shaytan) is to hinder the believer from reading Al-Quran. But during Ramadan Shaytan

2

himself is hindered from tempting the believer—for Al-Quran gives the reader the cherished privilege of directly conversing with the Creator of the Universe.

Thus, I included in this book discussions about the rules that are essential for reading and reciting Al-Quran. Indeed, the spiritual training during the month of Ramadan can not be complete without a great deal of reading of the Book of Allah. This divine Book deals with the questions of total life: creed, moral instructions, administration of warnings, giving good news, lessons from historical events, interpretation of the material and natural phenomenon, inviting humanity to their Maker, and admonishing the unbelievers. Al-Quran is an exposition on the spiritual as well as physical doctrine in which every verse and sentence has an intimate bearing on the other verse and sentence. Ramadan affords a believer an opportunity to cross-reference his entire life with the reading of Al-Quran; and anyone who observes this practice during Ramadan has a better chance of graduating to a higher level of faith.

The third pillar of Islam, Zakaat, is also discussed briefly and concisely in order to illustrate the basic Fiqh on Alms-giving. This is an opportunity that should not be lost on eligible Zakaat payers: to mix Ramadan with mandatory gift giving so as to carry on the commands of Allah (SWT) and to combat greed of an affluent person and to help the needy meet his essential needs, and thus build a bond of strong relationship in the Ummah.

Therefore, the *ESSENTIALS OF RAMADAN, THE FASTING MONTH* is a summary of the fundamental rules and laws on the Fiqh of Fasting, based on Al-Quran and the Sunnah of the Messenger (saas) to assist the reader in observing this special 'Ebadah of worship, as well as the traditionally related duties and obligations as mentioned earlier, Zakaat and the reading of Al-Quran. All praise be to Allah the Most High in the Beginning and in the End.

Tajuddin Bin Shu'aib
November 19, 1992/Ghumadal Awwal 25, 1413

GLOSSARY

عَامٌ

'AAM

Universal, prevalent and common. In Fiqh, it means the case has a general implication beyond its initial reason or cause. When the case is *'Aam* it covers the time, place and every believer. The opposite of *'aam* is *Khas*.

آدَابٌ

AADAB

From *Adaba*, cultured, well mannered. It implies rules or acts of *'Ebadah*. *Aadab* includes the dos and don'ts of fasting.

عَدْلٌ

'ADL

To act justly and fairly, from the root *'Adala*. In Fiqh, *'Aadl* is honesty, uprightness, impartiality, probity. All these are qualities required of a person who witnesses or testifies in any legal case, including testimony of sighting the new crescent for beginning or ending the month of Ramadan or any other month.

عَالِمٌ

'ALIM

Scholar, it is from the root word *'alim*, to know or to be recognized. An *alim* is a person who has dedicated himself to the letters and science of Islam, and has excelled in the sciences of Islam, *Ulumul Islam*, based in Al-Quran and the Hadith.

عَجْزٌ

'AJIZ

Incapable, from the root *'Ajaza*, lack of strength. It implies here a person who is incapable of carrying on the required duties in Islam. This person is not held responsible for caring on the Islamic duties.

عَقْلٌ

'AQIL

Sane, from *'aqil*, mind, brain. It is the person who is mentally sound and able. Sanity is the prerequisite of any act of worship.

4

اَرْكَانٌ

ARKAAN

Pillars, originally *rakana*, to learn, support one's own weight. The plural is *Arkaan*, principles, basic elements, basics. In fasting there are two *Arkaan*, intention and abstention.

عَاشُورَاه

'ASHURA

The tenth, originally *'ashrah*, ten. It denotes the tenth day of the month of Muharram. It is sunnah to fast on that day.

اللَّيْلُ

AL-LAYL

Night, we fast only during day time. There is no fasting at night.

أَيَّامُ التَّشْرِيقِ

AYYAMT-TASHRQ

These are the three days immediately following Eidul-Adha, the 11th, 12th and 13th of Dhul Hijjah. It is not desirable to fast during these days.

بَدْرٌ

BADIR

A full moon.

بِدْعَةٌ

BID'AH

Innovation, originally from *bada'a*, to start, invent, introduce. Here it is to innovate or invent something in the name of Islam as part of Islam, that has not been approved or sanctioned by Allah in *Al-Qur'an* or the Messenger of Allah in his Hadith. According to Hadith, every *Bid'ah* leads one astray, and every stray act leads to hellfire.

بَالِغٌ

BALIGH

Originally *balagha*, to reach, mature, ripen. Here it is the person who has reached the state of puberty. At this age the person is responsible for his or her acts. The state is known also as bulugh.

بُلُوغٌ

BULUGH

The state of puberty. It's synonym is *Hulum*, meaning the age of dreams, and *tamyeez*, the age of discretion.

دُعَاءٌ

DU'AA

Supplication.

عِبَادَةٌ

'EBADAH

From the root *'abada*, to worship, to serve, to venerate, to deify. Fasting is *Ebadah* (worship of Allah).

5

عِيدُ الْفِطْرِ
EIDUL-FITR

Fast-breaking festival on the first of Shawwal, the first day after Ramadan.

فَضَائِلُ
FADAIL

Virtues, from *fadala*, a surplus to excel, or surpass. *Fadail* refers to deeds of excellence, or deeds that promote moral excellence, virtues.

فَقِيةٌ
FAQEEH

Originally to comprehend, have knowledge. The plural is *fuqaha*. Legalist, jurisprudent, a scholar in the branch of Islamic science, *Fiqh*.

فَلَقٌ
FALAQ

Dawn.

فَطورٌ
FATUR

From *Fatara*, to split, or cleave, here to break the fast, eating food and drink after a fast.

فِعْلٌ
FI'EL

Deeds, it refers to a practical teaching of the Prophet (saas), as opposed to *quul*, spoken or verbal teachings of the Messenger.

حَيْضٌ
HAYD

Menstruation, monthly period. It invalidates many of the religious acts, including Salaat, fasting and touching the Book of Allah. If you miss a day or more of fasting due to *haid*, it has to be redeemed.

حَرِمٌ
HARIM

An old person. Age with debility is a determining factor whether a person can or cannot fast.

هِلاَلٌ
HILAL

Originally *halla*, to appear, show, as in a new moon. *Hilal* is the new moon, crescent, indicating the beginning of a new moon. Sighting or testimony of a new moon is the prerequisite of beginning the fast.

حِسَابٌ

HISAB

To determine and declare the beginning and the ending of the month by calculation and computation. This is an un-Islamic method for ascertaining the beginning and ending of Ramadan, for there is an explicit command to sight the new moon before the fast and to end the fast. There is an erroneous belief that calculation is a proof against error, but it is not pure science. There is near unanimity among the scholars regarding the fact that this is an incorrect way of testimony.

حُجَّةٌ

HUJJAH

Proof, from *hajja*, to overcome, to defeat, confute and convince. *Hujjah* is a proof, evidence, authoritative source to support a case. There is in Islamic *Shari'ah* a proof for everything. If the case lacks *Hujjah*, it is invalid.

حُكْمٌ

HUKUM

Hukum is a legal judgment. If someone asked you what is the *hukum* of a minors fasting, you may then respond to this question with the *hukum* saying the fasting of a minor is recommended. The *hukum* is to pass judgment, issue a verdict, or a sentence.

حُلُمٌ

HULUM

(Dream) We say youth has reached the age of *hulum*, referring to the wet dream, indicating he or she has reached puberty. This is synonymous to *bulugh* and *tamyeez*.

الإعْتِكَافُ

AL-I'ETIKAAF

From *'akafa*, to adhere, direct, to schedule, withdraw and retrieve. In Islamic fiqh term it is retirement to a Masjid for the worship of Allah. It is recommended to do this in the last ten days of Ramadan. However, it could be observed at any time provided it is in a Masjid.

إمْسَاكٌ

IMSAAK

Originally *masaka* to grab, seize and take hold. *Imsaak* is the time at which abstinence from things that break your fast begins, to mark the beginning time to fast. For instance, it is the time to start fasting in your locality.

إِمْسَاكِيَةٌ

IMSAAKIYAH The calendar of fasting during the month of Ramadan.

إِفْطَارٌ

IFTAAR To break fast. It is one of the *adaabs*, rules of fasting.

إِجْتِنَابٌ

IJTINAD Janaba, is the root word meaning to avert, keep away. Here it means avoidance of things that may invalidate fasting, especially spiritual fast-breakers, such as lies, bad-mouthing, etc.; things that are not in the spirit of fasting.

إِجْتِهَادٌ

IJTIHAD Originally *jahad*, to endeavor, strive, exert. *Ijtihad* is a judgment on a legal or theological question, based on the text in *Al-Quran* or Sunnah. Contrary to what many think, *Ijtihad* is a painstaking work based initially on Al-Quran and Hadith. It is considered one of the sources of Islamic *Shari'ah*.

إِخْتِلَافَ الْمَطَالِع

IKHITILAAFUL-MATALIE Phrase denoting differences of the crescent sighting. That is, the sighting of one region is not binding on the others. There are serious problems with this opinion or view due to the disagreement on what constitutes the difference.

إِتِحَادُالْمَطَالِع

ITHADUL-MATALIE A phrase meaning there is only one sighting of the crescent of Ramadan for Muslims all over the world. Therefore, if a Muslim in any region or locality, sights the *hilal*, and the testimony reaches Muslims any where in the world they should fast. This is the opinion of the majority of Muslim scholars.

جَمْهُورٌ

JAMHUR The majority of the scholars.

جَوَازٌ

JAWAAZ Originally *jaza*, to be allowed. *Jawaaz* means permissible, lawful, or an admissible act, such as taking a shower during Ramadan.

جِمَاعٌ

JIMAA Sexual relationship, it is a major fast-breaker.

8

جُـنَّةٌ

JUNNAH

Shield and protection, Ramadan acts as a *junnah*, shield for the faster.

كَافِرٌ

KAFIR

Originally to cover, hide. Here it means the person who hides the bounties of Allah, a disbeliever.

كَفَّارَةٌ

KAFFAARAH

Expiation for an irreligious act committed in violation of an Islamic Law.

مُفْطِرَاتٌ

MUFTIRAAT

Originally from *fatara*. To split or break. Here it denotes the acts or thing that invalidates fasting, such as eating, drinking, or sexual intercourse. The singular is *muftir*.

مُقِيمٌ

MUQEEM

The person who is staying, as opposed to traveling. Not traveling is a prerequisite of fasting, for the traveler is not obligated to fast.

مُكَلَّفٌ

MUKALLAF

Its root is *kalafa*, to become freckled, bent, set, be attached, commissioned, or entrusted. *Mukallah*, is the person who is commissioned, under obligation, liable or responsible, bound to observe the precepts of Islam. Every adult male or female Muslim is *Mukallaf*.

مَعْصِيَةٌ

MA'ASIYAII

From *'asa* to resist, oppose, defy, rebel. *Ma'asiyah* is a revolt against the tenets of the religion, known as sin. It is a *Ma'asiyah* to eat during the day time in Ramadan.

مَجْنُونٌ

MAJNOON

The person who is insane or mentally incompetent. A person in that state is not obligated to observe the rites of religion.

مَنْهِيَاتٌ

MANHIYAAT

Originally *naha* to forbid, ban, and interdict. *Manhiyaat* are the forbidden, interdicted or illicit deeds. Food and drink are *manhiyaat* during daytime but lawful at night during Ramadan.

مَصْلَحَةٌ

MASLAHAH

What is good and beneficial, from the root *salah*, to be good, right and proper. *maslahah* is an underlying reasoning behind all Islamic teachings in that there is always a *maslahu* behind every order, or precept of the religion.

مُتَابَعَةٌ

MUTABA'AH

Originally *tabia*, to follow, trail, and pursue. In *Shareeah*, it implies obeying and following the command of the Lawgiver. See the essence of *mutaba'ah*.

مُبَارِكٌ

MUBAARAK

Blessed, as in *Ramadan Mubaarak*, greeting the believers exchange during Ramadan and 'Eids as *'Eid Mubaarak*.

نَذِرٌ

NADHIR

To declare a vow. If you vow to fast certain days, you must fulfil your vow.

النِّيَةُ

NIYYAH

Intention.

النِّفَاسُ

NIFAAS

Post-childbirth bleeding. This bleeding is among the fast-breakers. During this period there is no fasting, but it has to be redeemed after Ramadan.

قَادِرٌ

QAADIR

To have strength, power. *Qaadir* means to be able to observe the religious obligations and rules. Ability is one of the prerequisites of fasting.

قَضَاءٌ

QADAA

To settle, and to finish. *Qadaa* is the redemption of a religious obligation, like redeeming Salaat that is missed, or making up a day, or days missed in fasting.

قَوْلِي

QAWLY

Originally to speak. The teachings of the Prophet (saas), that denotes what he says as opposed to deeds (fel). If the scholars of hadith say: this hadith is *Qawly*, they meaning the Prophet (saas) said it. If they say this hadith is *fiely* they mean he did it. For example, the Messenger said: "Whoever believes in Allah and the Day of Judgement either speak good or keep silent...." (Bukhari/Muslim)

الرَّوحُ

AR-RUUH

Breath of life, spirit, it is the Spirit of Allah. The angels and the spirits descend on the Night of Power. This is one of Angel Jibreel's names.

رَمَضَانُ

RAMADAN

The ninth month of Islamic calendar, and the fasting month.

الرَّيَّانُ

RAYYAN

Quencher, fragrance, a special gate in the heavens reserved only for those who fast in Ramadan. Originally, *rawiyah*, to drink one's fill. Quench, thus *rayyan* means the quencher, or a pleasant fragrance.

رُؤْيَةٌ

RUUYAH

Originally *Ra'a*, to see, discern, view. The method of testimony. Seeing, sighting, looking or viewing the new month (*hilaal*). Such as sighting the hilaal of Ramadan.

سَحُورٌ

SAHUUR

Originally *sahir*, lack of sleep, vigilance. Here it means the meal taken before dawn, just before beginning a day's fast.

صَوْمٌ

SAWM

Generally, it denotes restraining from normal things such as eating, drinking, etc. In Islamic law (*Sharee'ah*), it means special acts of worship, i.e. fasting with intention to please Allah by abstaining from fast-breakers such as food, drink, and sexual intercourse from the period between the break of dawn until sundown.

صَومُ الدَّهْر

SAUMD-DAHAR

Dahar, is time, lifetime, epoch, eternity. It is to fast for the entire year without break. This kind of fasting is un-Islamic.

صَدَقَةُ الْفِطْرِ

SADAQATUL FITR

Fast-breaking charity to be given at the end of Ramadan. This is a special charity, consisting of giving food items.

سَفَرٌ

SAFAR

Travel, and *musaafir* is a traveller.

صَحِيحٌ

SAHIH

Authentic, originally to be healthy, well, sound, perfect. In the *Fiqh* of *'Ebadat* it refers to a valid act that is approved or sanctioned by the Lawgiver. It denotes also the category of hadith, as in Sahih Bukhari and Muslim.

صَائِمٌ صَائِمَةٌ

SAAIM/SAAIMAH

From *sama*, one who fasts; the female is *Saimah*.

ﷺ

SAAS

Abbreviated letters which stand for *Sallallahu Alaihi Wa Sallam*. It is the prayer we are commanded to say when the name of Prophet Muhammad is mentioned.

شَفَاعَةٌ

SHAFAAH

Shafa'ah, to attach, add, subjoin, intercede, to mediate. In a Hadith fasting will intercede for the faster.

شَهِدَ

SHAHIDA

To bear witness, as in witnessing and testifying to the sighting of the new crescent.

شَامٌ

SHAAMM

The historical name describing the geographical region that refers to the countries of Syria, occupied Palestine, Jordan, and Lebanon.

شَهْرٌ

SHAHAR

A month in Arabic as in shahar Ramadan.

شَرِيعَةٌ

SHARI'AH or
SHAREE'AH

Islamic jurisprudence, law. From *shara'a*, to commence, begin. *Shariah* in Arabic denotes a water source, drinking fountain. Here it means Islamic jurisprudence; the embodiment of a revealed message, or canonical law of Al-Islam, based in Al-Quran and the Sunnah.

شَرِبَ

SHARIBA

To drink.

الشَّارِعُ

SHAARI'E

The Lawgiver. In Islam the Lawgiver is Allah (SWT), and His Messenger Prophet Muhammad (saas). Allah is Shaarie because He is the Creator; and Prophet Muhammad is Lawgiver because Allah permitted him to give law on His behalf by the virtue of his messengership. Therefore, these two entities are the makers of the laws that govern the life of a Muslim and all human beings from the time prophet Muhammad came to be seen until the end of time.

سُبْحَانَهُ وَ تَعَالَى

SWT

Abbreviation letters denoting the Sublime name of Almighty Allah, (S) *Subhaanahu* (Glory be to Allah), (W) and (T) *Ta'ala* (The Exalted).

سِتُ مِنْ شَوَّالِ

**SITT MIN
SHAWWAL**

The six days of Shawwal. Shawwal is the tenth month of the Islamic calendar. This refers to a highly recommended Sunnah six days fasting in Shawwal after Ramadan.

سِرُ

SIRR

Secret, innermost thoughts, originally from *sarra*. The plural is *asrar*. In every *'Ebadah* there is hidden wisdom, the discovery of which enriches belief and conviction. Fasting is replete with hidden insights (*asrar*) that our scholars past and present are still discovering.

السُّنَةُ الْمُؤَكَدَةُ

SUNNAH MU'AQADAH

Sunnah, from *sanna* to introduce, enact, prescribe, indent, to pass a law. Here it is the teaching of the Messenger of Allah, (saas), including what he said, did, or approved. *Muaqadah* means strong, thus when Sunnah is described as Muaqadah, it indicates the Messenger observed the act frequently.

طَعَامٌ

TAAAM

Food.

تَعَمُّدٌ

TA'AMMUD

'Amida is the root word meaning to intend, undertake. Here it means deliberate, intentional and willful disregard of the precepts of Islam, such as eating in the middle of the day in the month of Ramadan. Its opposite is *sahaw*, unintentional.

تَقْلِيدٌ

TAQLID

Originally, *qalada*, to confer, adorn with a necklace, to copy, to imitate. *Taqled* is to follow, or imitate blindly, or not questioning the adoption of concepts or ideas. Uncritical faith.

تَمْرٌ

TAMUR

The date, fruit.

تَوَاتُرٌ

TAWAATUR

A term used in the science of hadith to describe a hadith which has been reported overwhelmingly through several chains *(Sanad or Asaaneed)*, as opposed to *Ahaad* the one reported through a single chain *(Sanad)*.

عُمْرَةٌ

UMRAH

The lesser Hajj. It is highly recommended during Ramadan.

وُجُوبٌ

WUJUUB

From *wajaba*, to be necessary, indispensable. *Wujuub* is an obligatory act, it is similar to *wajib*, necessary and essential.

اِلزَّكَاةُ

ZAKAAT

Alms, the third pillar of Al-Islam. It is highly recommended to give Zakaat during Ramadan.

Essentials of Ramadan, the Fasting Month

FASTING (*SIYAAM*)

Fasting, *siyaam*, has two meanings. Generally, siyaam or *sawm*, is derived from the root sama, to restrain from normal things, such as eating, drinking, and talking. If an individual refrains from these things, he is considered *saaim*, the observer of fast. Al-Qur'an uses the word generally when it revealed the conversation between the angel and Mary, the mother of Jesus, as the angel instructed her: "...And if you do see any man, say, 'I have vowed to remain silent for Allah.'" (*Al-Qur'an 19:26*)

The phrase "to remain silent" is the interpretation of the Arabic word, "*sawm*." The reason for this interpretation is that "*sawm*" cannot mean fast, i.e. restraint from food, because Mary had just been told to eat from the palm tree. This general meaning is common in the Arabic language.

In the Shari'ah (Islamic law) the "*sawm*" means and implies a specific act, which is, "To worship Allah, abstaining, with intention to please Him from fast breakers, such as physical nourishment, food, drink, and sexual intercourse or a lustful discharge of semen from the period between the break of dawn until sundown."

As this definition implies, the Islamic fasting is total abstinence from any food particles passing through the mouth or nose, as well as drinks of any kind — water, milk, juices, etc. — along with abstinence from sexual association during the day that commences from the break of dawn till sunset.

Although the definition indicates restraining the stomach and private parts, the tongue, eyes, ears and other limbs are equally obligated to be restrained if the faster wants to gain the total rewards of fasting. This is why the Messenger of Allah (saas) has been reported as saying in a hadith by Abu Hurairah:

"He who does not desist from obscene language and acting obscenely (during the period of fasting), Allah has no need that he did not eat or drink." (Bukhari Muslim)

In another hadith by abu Harairah (raa), the Prophet (saas) said: "Fasting is not only to restrain from food and drink, fasting is to refrain from obscene (acts). If someone verbally abuses you or acts ignorantly towards you, say (to them) 'I am fasting; I am fasting.'" (Ibn Khuzaimah)

Indeed, these two reports imply fasting will not be complete until one observes three elements:

1. Restraining the stomach and the private parts from the breakers of the fast-food and drink,

2. restraining the *jawarih*, the other body parts, which may render the fast worthless despite the main factors of hunger and thirst; so the tongue, for instance, must avoid backbiting, slander, and lies; the eyes should avoid looking into things considered by the Lawgiver as unlawful; the ears must stop from listening to conversations, words, songs, and lyrics that spoil the spirit of fasting; and,

3. restraining of the heart and mind from indulging themselves in other things besides *dhikir Allah* (remembrance of Allah).

THE MERITS OF FASTING

Islam is built on five pillars. Each represents a unique utility, an institution, if you will, through which the believer builds his relationship with the Creator and the creation. Of all the pillars of Islam, none is more special than siyaam, fasting. While there may be an appearance of *riya*, eye service, or show, in all other pillars—Salaat, Zakaat, Hajj, and even the *Kalimah*—there is no such possibility in fasting. The only One who knows that you are really abstaining is Allah, the Almighty. It is easy to pretend to be fasting; while in hiding, you may eat or drink. Thus, fasting is considered a special worship, as Hadith reports from the Messenger of Allah (saas) have detailed.

It has been reported by the way of Abu Hurairah (raa) that the Prophet (saas) reported that Allah (SWT) said in a Hadith Al-Qudsi: "All services of the son of Adam are for him except fasting. It is for Me, and I will reward him for it. Fasting is a shield. On the day you fast, do not use obscenity, nor yell at others, nor act ignorantly towards them. However, if anyone abuses you verbally or attempts to draw you to fight with him, say 'I am fasting' two times. The Prophet (saas) then states: I swore by the One (Allah) in Whose Hand is the soul of Muhammad, the breath of the faster is sweeter to Allah on the Day of Judgment than the scent of musk. The faster experiences enjoyment twice: he is pleased when he breaks his fast, and he is pleased when he meets his Maker" (Muslim)

Among the points this incisive hadith revealed is that fasting is Allah's. Certainly, there is only one reason why a believer will put himself or herself through this trying physical exercise and that is to seek the pleasure of Allah (SWT). The fast is the single most important device to test the *Iman*, faith, of the believer and the depth of his sincerity and commitment to the concept of *Tauheed*, the Oneness of Allah.

The hadith also states that fasting is a shield, an armor protecting the believer from sinful acts *(ma'asi)*. Do you not know that nourishment is the first culprit in the propagation of sins? For when you eat, the blood flow increases considerably, and the energy level increases, making it easier for Satan to use your own energy level to tempt you to commit sins. In another hadith, the Prophet states: "Satan runs in the circulatory system of the son of Adam in the same way blood circulates in our system; so tighten his passages with hunger." (Bukhari/Muslim)

Now you see why fasting becomes a shield. Fasting enables the believer to guard against his archenemy. It also helps him against human evil by putting the patience and perseverance gained from fasting into use with forbearance and forgiveness of the attacker—that is, of course, when the safety of ones life is not involved. Otherwise, in this case, Al-Qur'an allows the believer to repel evil without transgression.

BAD BREATH

The above Hadith also gives the faster good news regarding the changing breath of the faster, which is sweeter to Allah (SWT) than musk. The changing breath of the mouth is a vivid physical testimony of this discipline. As much as we hate bad breath, in fasting it is a good thing, for it is caused by the coating which appears on the upper surface of the tongue soon after the commencement of the fast. After desiring food, the body begins to digest such waste material and deposits of fat as are available to it. This coating on the tongue is an outward proof that inner elimination is in progress. As soon as the digestive organs have been purified, the mouth returns to normal.

In a hadith related by Abdullah Bin 'Umar, the Prophet said: "Fasting (Siyaam) and the Book of Allah (Al-Qur'an) will intercede for the servant on the Day of Judgment. The fasting will say: 'O, Allah, I denied him nourishment and sex during the daytime. Let me intercede on his behalf,' and Al-Qur'an will say: 'I denied him sleep during night time; so let me intercede on his behalf.' So Allah will allow them to intercede on his behalf." (Ahmed)

This hadith indicates on the Day of Judgment, when the events will be overwhelming and the outcome uncertain, the fast and the Book will intercede for the servants of Allah. As every second of daytime devotion and every letter of Al-Qur'an voices their pleasure openly with you during the witnessing and interviewing, bear in mind that *shafa'ah* (intercession), is an extreme privilege and a rare commodity. Even the average prophet will not attempt to intercede for anyone on this day.

Shal bin Sa'ad reported the Messenger of Allah (saas) said: "Paradise *(Jannah)* has a door called *Rayyan* (the quencher), which is preserved for those who observed fasting on the Day of Judgment. It will be announced, 'Where are those who observed fasting?' The door, Rayyan, will not be closed until the last one of them enters." (Bukhari and Muslim)

This is what the pleasure of Allah is all about. The person who observes fasting becomes an elite in the hour that every other person is busy turning the pages of their books of deeds. This is the time you are pulled away through the *rayyan* Gate to Paradise.

Abu Sa'eed Al-Khudree related the Messenger of Allah (saas) said: "If a servant of Allah fasts a day for the pleasure of Allah (SWT), He will distance his face from the hellfire, in the equivalent of that day, which, in the sight of Allah, will take seventy years to cover." (Bukhari/Muslim)

The Hereafter is real, and rewarding evil in kind is also real; but as a reward to those who observe the fast, Allah (SWT) will distance them from the ultimate punishment. These four reports underscore the spiritual as well as the physical value of Siyaam, fasting.

KINDS OF FASTING

Fasting is divided into two kinds: Fard, the obligatory fast, and Tatau'u, non-obligatory fast. The obligatory fast is categorized as three kinds:

(1) fasting the month of Ramadan

(2) fasting to expiate for religious offenses

(3) fasting to fulfill a vow

Of the three, fasting the month of Ramadan is the most important; so we will devote most of the discussion to it in our book.

FASTING THE MONTH OF RAMADAN— *SAWM RAMADAN*

When we speak of Ramadan, we speak of an annual spiritual event so serious that it impressively engulfs the entire Muslim Ummah in a religious season surpassing any annual event in the world.

Ramadan is the ninth month in the Islamic calendar, Al-Hijrah. This calendar is based on the lunar system. There are twelve months in the lunar year, They are:

1. Al-Muharram	7. Rajab
2. Safar	8. Sha'aban
3. Rabee'ul Awwal	9. Ramadan
4. Rabee'ul Athanthanee	10. Shawwal
5. Jumadah Awwal	11. Dhul-Qidah
6. Jumadth Thanee	12. Dhul-Hijah

WHAT IS RAMADAN?

Ramadan is derived from the Arabic root word *ramida* or *ar-ramad* intense scorching heat and dryness, especially the ground. From the same root there is ramdaa, sunbaked sand, and the famous proverb: *"Kal Mustajeer minar Ramadaa binnar"* — to jump out of the frying pan into the fire. And in a hadith the Messenger of Allah (saas) said: "The prayer of repenters is due when the young camel can feel the sun's heat early in the morning." (Muslim)

Thus, the Ramadan is so called to indicate the heating sensation in the stomach as a result of thirst. Others said it is so called because Ramadan scorches out the sins with good deeds, as the sun burns the ground. Some said it is so called because the hearts and souls are more readily receptive to the admonition and remembrance of Allah during Ramadan, as the sand and stones are receptive to the sun's heat. The framers of this beautiful language may have been inspired by Allah (SWT) in naming this month Ramadan. Otherwise, the relation between the heat and its properties is miraculously similar to that of Ramadan. While the heat represents the matter that helps shape, form, and mold virtually every matter — from metal and plastics, to plants and living cells — Ramadan undoubtedly helps a serious believer remold, reshape, reform, and renew his physical and spiritual disposition and behavior.

LEGAL STATUTES OF RAMADAN

The observation of Ramadan is mandated by two Islamic sources, Al-Qur'an and Sunnah, along with *Ijmaa*, the consensus of the scholars. Al-Qur'an states: "O, you who believe fasting is prescribed to you, as it was prescribed to those before you that you may acquire self-restraint." *(Al-Qur'an 2:183)*

The proof in this citing is very obvious, for whenever Allah (SWT) uses the word *kutiba*, which means, among other things, prescribed or written, it indicates the action that follows it becomes mandatory upon the believers, men and women. After establishing *Sawm*, the verse emphasized that this was not the first time the obligation of fasting had been established, for it stated that previous nations received the same mandate. We are not certain about the time, date, and amount.

Many scholars state the introductory clause "as it was" *kamaa* in the verse above implies and refers to the analogy between our

fasting today and the fasting of previous people. There are simi-
larities in the time and amount, but what happened to Ramadan
in years past is that the high priests, before the time of Prophet
Muhammad (saas) added more days than were prescribed for
them. It became difficult and they could not do it, so they moved
the date to spring until they neglected it altogether.

In a hadith it is reported by Daghfal Imam Hanzalah (raa) that
the Messenger of Allah (saas) said: "The Christians used to fast
one month. So when a man fell ill amongst them, they vowed if
Allah cured him, they would increase ten more days to their fasting. He was cured, and the fast became *forty days*. Then another
man ate meat; his stomach pained him. They vowed again if
Allah cured him, they would add seven more days. He was cured
and the fast increased to *forty-seven days*."

Then a king fell ill. They vowed again if Allah cured him, they
would complete seven to ten days and move their fast to the
spring. The king was cured and the fast increased to *fifty days*."
(Tafseer Al-Qurtabi)

This is how the pillar of religion was neglected. Even some
Christian writer complained, "For nearly a century and a half,
fasting has been out of vogue, at least in the churches of the West.
The very idea of someone actually fasting today seems strange to
most twentieth century Christians. They associate it with medieval Christianity." (Fasting a Neglected Discipline)

Some said the analogy is referring to the manner of fasting—
restraint from food and drink and marital relations. The verse
(2:183) ends with a strong hint to the spiritual benefit of fasting:
"That ye may acquire self-restraint." The word used is *tataqun*. It is
originally from *waqa*, to protect, the same base word used for fear
of Allah, *taqwa*; for when you fear Allah, you protect yourself
against His wrath and against things that will destroy yourself.

Taqwa (fear of Allah), is easily achieved with fasting for the
simple reason that, when you fast, you become weak for the lack
of nourishment, which means your cravings are diminished.
With diminished cravings, the sins are greatly lessened, because
there is no energy to fuel them, praise be to Allah. When sin is
lessened, the barometer for *taqwah* rises.

Elsewhere Allah (SWT) states: "Ramadan is the month in
which was sent down the Qur'an as a guide to humanity and as a
clear sign for guidance and judgment (between right and wrong).

So anyone of you who witnesses the month should spend it in fasting..." *(Al-Qur'an, 2:185)*

This verse contains important rules and reasons for fasting that will be explained later. However, what concerns us here is the statement, "So anyone of you who witnesses the month should spend it in fasting." There are exceptions, like when traveling, which will be explained later also.

The above examples have been given as the proof from in Al-Qur'an. As for the proof from hadith, there are many, amongst them a hadith reported by Bukhari and Muslim in which the Messenger (saas) states: "Islam is built on five (pillars), testimony that there is no deity worthy of worship but Allah, and testimony that Muhammad is His messenger, establishing Salat, giving Zakaat, observing the fast of Ramadan, and pilgrimage to the House of Allah." (Bukhari/Muslim)

The hadith established fasting during the month of Ramadan as one of the pillars on which this religion is built. This hadith reinforces the obligation of fasting as stated in Al-Qur'an. We will see later that there are other Hadiths that explain in detail how to observe the *'Ebadah*, the worship of fasting.

Because of this collection of proofs from both Al-Qur'an and the Sunnah, the Muslim scholars agreed in *Ijima'a* that abstinence from physical nourishment and sex associated with intention to seek Allah's pleasure is mandatory upon every believer. Before verse (2:185) was revealed, Muslims were commanded to fast three days in every month (verse 2:183). This verse (2:185) was revealed on Monday, Sha-aban 2, in the second year of Hijrah, thus, abrogating the earlier order.

MERITS OF RAMADAN

When we speak of the merits of something *(fadl* or *fadail)*, we are actually saying the deeds in it are highly recommended and the reward and benefits highly emphasized and guaranteed. I would like to cite several *Ahadith* that address this issue of *fadaill*, merits of fasting during Ramadan, and filling the entire month with more'ebadah than any other month.

Abu Hurairah (raa) relates the Messenger of Allah (saas) said when one Ramadan came:

"A blessed month has arrived. Observing it in fasting is mandated on you (the believers). During this month, the gates of

Paradise will be opened and the gates of Hellfire will be closed. The evil ones (*Shayaatin*) will be handcuffed. In it there is one night, during which worship is better than worship in a thousand months. Whoever is denied its blessings has been denied the biggest blessing." (Ahmed, Nasaae, and Bayhaqi)

This hadith is similar to the previous one, except that it emphasizes the importance of being mindful and aware of the rules that govern the *'ebadah* of fasting. For one of the key words in every *'ebadah* is "*muwafaqah Ash-Shari'ie*," observing in accordance to the commands of the Lawgiver.

NEGLECTING RAMADAN

The blessed month of Ramadan comes once in a lunar calendar year for serious spiritual and physical training and rehabilitation of the believers. To neglect this Islamic obligation, with all its benefits, is a serious, and unpardonable sin. Thus the warning from the Prophet (saas). Abu Hurairah reports the Messenger of Allah said: "Whoever breaks one day's fast of Ramadan without an authorized permission from Allah, he will never be able to redeem it (with another) day's fast, even if he fasts to eternity." (Tirmidhi)

The stern warning in this hadith for breaking fast in Ramadan is an indication of how serious the offense is perceived by the Shari'e, the Lawgiver. You may think that if you break a day, you can redeem it after Ramadan. Indeed, the missed day may be redeemed after Ramadan, but the hadith indicates that fasting for a lifetime (*Siyaam Dahr*), or to eternity cannot make up for the spiritual loss due to a reckless and deliberate break of a fasting day. It is abhorrent to neglect an Islamic rite which is your duty, but worse to neglect an obligation that belongs to Allah (SWT), such as the fast of Ramadan.

ASCERTAINING THE CRESCENT OF RAMADAN (HILAL)

Ever since the Lawgiver (*Shaari'e*) prescribed fasting, the method and the process of ascertaining the knowledge about the starting and the ending time of fasting has been to physically sight (*ru'eyah*) the new crescent moon (*hilal*) of Ramadan. Thus, when the birth of the new moon of the month of Ramadan is ascertained, the fast begins. The fast ends with the birth of the hilal of the tenth month, Shawwal. In the event that clouds, smog, or fog block the sky, preventing eye sighting of the hilal, we compute the days of the month. If after, or on the evening of, the twenty-ninth day of Sha'aban, we are unable to sight the hilal of Ramadan, due to cloudiness or obstruction in the sky, we will complete Sha'aban thirty days, and the fast begins the next morning. Similarly, if after the 29th of Ramadan, we are unable to sight the hilal of Shawwal due to cloudiness or obstruction, we complete Ramadan 30 days. The next day becomes *'Eidul Fitr*, the Festival of Fast-Breaking.

Thus, the question of ascertaining the birth of the new Hilal crescent before commencing and ending the fast is born out in this verse, where Allah, the Almighty, says: "Whoever is present during the month should spend it in fasting..." *(Al-Qur'an 2:185)*

Most translators of Al-Qur'an interpreted the key word in this verse, *shahida*, to mean 'to be present' so as to exclude the traveler, for he does not have to fast. That is very interesting because, if shahida is general, *al-'aam*, there should be more than one case to exclude; for, we would have to exclude the sick, minors, the insane, as well as the traveler. All these categories will be present, but yet fasting will not be mandatory for some of them.

The word *shahida* should be translated "whoever witnesses or gives testimony." This will leave the verse's general meaning intact, then exclude from it whoever deserves to be excluded.

The verse *(aayat)* "whoever witnesses..." is a conditional clause and the condition is ascertaining the hilal, with fasting as the result. That is to say, if there is no witness, there is no fasting. The word for month is *shahr*. Linguistically it means crescent; so it indicates whoever witnesses any part of the crescent should observe the entire month in fasting.

This is the ruling of the most recognized Muslim scholars of Tafseer, Hadith and Fiqh. The basis for this ruling is derived from several ahadith, which are overwhelmingly reported *(Tawatur)*.

Ibn Umar (raa) reported, "During the time of the Prophet (saas), the companions went looking for the new crescent. So I told the Prophet (saas) that I saw it. So he fasted and told the companions to fast." (Abu Dahud / Hakim)

This hadith indicates the process of hilal testimony, the believers should go out and ascertain the new hilal. It indicates also when and how. As for when, that has been explained, but I would like to add the legal sighting time begins on the 29th of the month, because unlike the Gregorian calendar, where the days of the month are fixed, in the lunar calendar (Hijrah) they are not. For instance, Sha'aban this year may be 29 days; next year it may be 30.

As for the process of testimony (shahidah), it should commence soon before sunset or soon after, while there is still some light in the sky, for the Hilal does not remain in the horizon very long.

How does one ascertain the hilal? The testimony of hilal can be achieved by (a) direct sighting, where you see it yourself, or (b) indirect sighting, where someone sees it, and you rely on his sighting.

If an individual who is reliable, upright, and trustworthy ('adl) witnesses the hilal, it becomes incumbent upon him to fast. If he informs others about his testimony, according to the majority of the scholars, it becomes incumbent upon them to fast. This is the ruling that enjoys support in hadith.

The hadith poses a Fiqh question. That is: the testimony of how many people would be enough? The minimum, according to the hadith is one person who is 'Adl. The Messenger of Allah (saas) fasted and commanded the believers to do likewise, depending solely on the testimony of one person, Abdullah bin 'Umar. This is the opinion of the majority of the scholars, which is near consensus. However, in the case of sighting the hilal of Shawwal to end Ramadan, some said the minimum is two or more.

This leads to disagreement among the scholars who debate whether the testimony of one individual is valid to break Ramadan. Some said because this is the ending of Ramadan, there should be two witnesses instead of one. But the problem with this opinion is that there is no proof to substantiate it and, hence, no base for it. In the absence of proof (dalil), it remains that one person's witness is enough to end the fasting.

Abu Hurairah (raa) related that the Messenger of Allah (saas) said: "Fast by sighting the (new) hilal, and break your fast by sighting. If there is a cloud, complete the counting of Sha'aban 30 days." (Bukhari and Muslim)

The hadith of Ibn 'Umar (raa) is a hadith of action (fi'el), how the Prophet (saas) acted, that is, physical search of the edges of the horizon to ascertain the testimony. The hadith of Abu Hurairah is the hadith of saying, (qawl). Thus, both are commands by action and commands by a verbal expression employed to instruct the believers about the process of sighting hilal. This should have made the case for starting and ending Ramadan. But this is not the case. There is always a dispute among the believers.

One age-old controversy is whether we should go by the order of the Lawgiver or should we depend on calculations. The truth of the matter is that there are two opinions, one the majority and the other the minority opinion. The latter has no proof whatsoever to substantiate their opinion except one word in the other version of the hadith. The Prophet (saas) said: *faqdiru*, meaning if it be cloudy, measure or estimate it. The minority opinion says this is a proof that calculations can be used. The majority says the word *faqdiru* is ambiguous. It has been explained in a hadith narrated by Abu Hurairah, which states, *"fa ak milu al-edah,"* complete the account. They added, "if the Lawgiver *(Shaari'e)* wanted us to use calculation, he would have just forgotten about the original ordinance regarding sighting before fasting and sighting before ending." In the Tafseer of Al-Qurtabi, Ibn Nafi'e (ra) reported that Imam Malik bin Anas (ra) said: "If you see an Imam who does not begin and end fasting by way of sighting, but begins fasting by calculation, he should not be followed in prayer or emulated." The renowned scholar Ibn Al'Arabi said, "Some of our people erred when they reported that Imam Shaf'e relied on calculations." Ibn Al-'Arabi commented, "The report is baseless and falsehood." (Al-Qurtabi)

INTERNATIONAL SIGHTING

Another point that arises out of the hadith of Abu Hurairah is whether the sighting of one region is good for the sighting of the whole Ummah; i.e., should a New Yorker depend on the sighting of *hilal* in Paris? There is a difference of opinions on this subject. The reason for this dispute is due to a report *(athar)* from Ibn Abbas. If I may state, there are differences between the hadith from the Prophet (saas) and *(athar)* a report from a companion. So this report is not the same as hadith.

In this *athar*, Kuraib (raa) reported that: "Umm Al-Fadl sent him to Mu'awiyah in Shaam (Damascus). As he finished his business and was preparing to return to Medina, the *hilal* of Ramadan was sighted in the *Shaam* area on Friday night, and people started to fast the next day. As he arrived home in Medina at the end of Ramadan, Ibn Abbas (raa) asked him about his trip. Then they talked about the *hilal*. 'When did they see it,' Ibn 'Abbas asked. Kuraib informed Ibn Abbas that they saw it Friday night. Abdullah Ibn Abbas wanted to know whether he himself saw the *hilal*. Kuraib replied, 'Yes, as well as many people. They fasted, and Mu'awaiyah, too, fasted.' Ibn Abbas said 'But we saw it Saturday night, and we will continue to fast until we complete thirty days or see it.' Kuraib asked him, 'Aren't you satisfied with the testimony of Mu'awiyah and his fasting?' 'No,' Ibn Abbas replied. He continued, 'That is what the Messenger of Allah commanded us to do.'" (Bukhari/Muslim)

This *athar* is the base text used by the minority, who ruled that the people in each region should sight their own *hilal*. Then they disagreed among themselves.

(1) Some said every town and city has its own exclusive testimony in that its sighting is not binding on other towns. For instance, sighting in Los Angeles is valid only for the residents of that city, and not valid in San Diego. The testimony in New York City is valid for the New Yorkers and not valid for the residents of Buffalo.

(2) Every town has its exclusive testimony; however, the difference between this and the previous point is that the ruler or the governor can demand that people under his order and in his territorial influence fast according to the sighting of other towns, for to him all the towns are one under his command.

(3) The countries in close proximity depend on each other's testimony. The countries which are far apart, do not. For instance, the testimony in New York City is not valid in Los Angeles, but it may be allowed for the East coast cities.

(4) Some say it depends on the region. For instance, people in the eastern region will have one exclusive testimony as opposed to people in the western region, southern, and/or northern regions.

(5) The last opinion is that of the *Jamhur* (the majority of scholars). They said the differences of regions, distances and terrain are of no consequence in determining the testimony of the crescent. The only consideration is the sighting. If the testimony of the *hilal* is ascertained by even one believer in any part of the world, he or she is obligated to begin the fast. The proof is the direct testimony of the Messenger of Allah (saas), who said: "Fast by sighting the *hilal* and break by sighting." (Bkhari/Muslim)

This, the *Jamhuur* said, is an address (khitab), to all Muslims. The testimony of any one Muslim is testimony for all Muslims.

As for the Kuraib report, they explained that it is not proof in the order or strength of the above hadith. It is a known fact among the scholars of Islamic jurisprudence that a report from *Sahabi* (a companion), *Tabi'een* (the followers of the companions), and *Tabi'e al-tabi'een* (the followers of the followers of the companions), and the *Ulama* (scholars) cannot be used independently as proof and evidence *(hujjah)*. It will be evidence only if the report is direct from the Messenger of Allah and not their independent judgment opinion *(Ijtihad)* what they infer or deduce from what The Prophet said. The Kuraib report is in that latter category, i.e., Ibn 'Abbas making Ijtihad, "This the Messenger of Allah commanded us." For that which the Messenger of Allah commanded is the direct Hadith reported in the books of hadith, such as Bukhari, Muslim, and many others:

"Do not fast until you see the crescent, and do not break fast until you see the crescent; but if there are clouds, complete the calculation of thirty days." (Bukhari/Muslim)

This hadith does not specify one region from the other. Instead, it addresses Muslims in general all over the globe. Because this hadith is general, "*Aam*," it will not be made specific "*khaas*" without another direct hadith from the Prophet (saas), and there is none. If there is no evidence from the Kuraib report, what then is the reason for Abdullah bin Abbas's, (raa) refusal to fast according to the sighting in Shaam? The reason is his *Ijtihad*, independent judgment, that the distance between the two regions, Medina and Shaam, are far apart and large to the extent that each should have its own independent sighting.

This *Ijtihad* at best is very weak because it is well known that countries and towns do depend on each other's witnesses and information from all Islamic Sharee'ah cases, and undoubtedly moon-sighting is one of them. Ibn Abbas did not state the text from the Prophet (saas) nor did he state the deduction from any text.

Further examination of this report unfortunately reveals that the only evidence he states is the general opinion that Medinians do not depend on the testimony of Shaamians. Indeed, if we accept Kuraib's report, it will mean that Muslims in one region will have difficulty beginning the fast of Ramadan in unity. Thus, international sighting is the correct interpretation and ruling as advanced by the majority of Muslims scholars.

Logistically, it would have being impossible for Ibn Abbaas (raa) to fast according to the sighting of Shaam even if he wanted to for the simple reason that, during that period, it takes express mail seven days from Shaam to Madinah. Were Ibn Abbaas decided to follow shaam he and the people of Madinah would have to wait seven days to start or end Ramadan. There were no communication devices such as telephones, faxes and telegrams. Many scholars believe that if Ibn Abbaas were in position to know that on the eve of Ramadan or Eid, crescent has been sighted in Shaam, he would have started fasting or end the fasting. Therefore, the *athar (the report of Kuraib)* would be used only if groups of believers find themselves in a town or country in which they are totally cut off from the outside world. No city today can claim that. Allah is the best knower.

WHAT SHOULD BE SAID AT THE SIGHTING OF THE CRESECENT

It is recommended that whoever sights the crescent (Hilal) of Ramadan, or any other month for that matter, or being informed about the new crescent, should say:

Allahu Akbar, Allahumma ahillahu'alaina bil yumni wa Iman, Was Salaamata wal Islam, Ribbi wa rabbika Allah. (Tirmidhi)	(Meaning) Allah is Greatest. O Allah, make it the beginning, the beginning of prosperity, faith, peace, and total submission to Allah. Your Lord and mine is Allah.

Also, it has been reported from Ali bin Abi Talib (raa) that the Messenger said: "If you witness the crescent of the new month, say:

Allahu Akbar (three times)	Allah is Greatest (three times)
Al-hamdu Lillah, Alladhi	praise be to Allah who created me
Khalaqani wa Khalaqaka, wa	and you and decreed for you the
qaddara laka manajil wa	phases and made you a sign for
ja'alaka ayatna lil'ala meen."	the universe.
(Naylul Awataar)	

BASIC ELEMENTS OF FASTING

There are two basic elements that constitute the essence of Islamic fasting. The observation of these elements makes one's fasting acceptable.

The first element of fasting is abstinence of fast-breakers from the break of dawn *(fajr)* until sunset. For the fast-breakers, the Lawgiver, meant in no uncertain terms and free from any ambiguity and confusion, abstinence from food and drink and sexual relations. Any nourishment taken by mouth or nose, or drink of any sort, water, juices, milk, etc., should be avoided. Also, sexual intercourse during daytime is prohibited.

In this element, the period of observance is daily. It is not Islamic fasting when fasting takes place at night. Indeed, we are encouraged to break the fast without any delay as soon as the sun goes down. The proof for this first element is the saying of the Most High: "...And now associate with them and seek what Allah has ordained for you and eat and drink until the white thread of dawn appears to you distinct from its black thread." *(Al-Quran 2:187)*

This verse defines the time limits in which the worshiper is obligated to exercise abstinence. The first part of the verse is an indication of Allah's mercy upon the worshipers by making it easy for them during night hours in their relations with their spouses. For when verse (2:185) was revealed, it restricted daily as well as nightly relations with spouses. It was obviously difficult for the believers.

Imam Al-Qurtabi and others reported: 'Umar bin Al-Khataab (raa) returned home late at night after visiting the Prophet (saas). When he came home, he felt the urge for his wife, so he slept with his wife, breaking the rule. Early in the morning he went to the Prophet (saas) and informed him about the incident. He said, "I seek pardon from Allah and you. My soul tempted me to have relations with my wife. Can you find a permission for me in this offense?" The Prophet, (saas), asked whether he really was serious about this. 'Umar (raa) replied, 'Yes.' The Prophet (saas) did not have an answer for him, but told him Allah has to decide on this.

By the grace of Allah, before 'Umar arrived home, Allah (SWT) revealed verse (2:187), permitting believers to enjoy their wives during the night. So this is what the verse is referring to. It sets the limit of abstinence. It does so in metaphorical language draped with flair and beauty, as it describes the starting and the ending time of fast. Eat and drink until the white thread, i.e., the first rays of light finds its way through the horizon, the black thread. At that time, one must stop eating and start the observance of fasting.

The second element of fasting is *niyyah* (intention). In Islamic practices, *niyyah* is highly rated. This remarkable element is not unique to fasting; it permeates every ounce of the believer's undertakings from *Salaat*, to *Zakaat*, to *Hajj*. It is the difference between whether the actions are religious or irreligious. For instance, fasting for political reasons, or as a weapon of passive resistance, or hunger strikes, or starving for dietary reasons, or weight control, or even on medical advice—all of these are not proper Islamic fasting, because they lack one main component: that is, the *niyyah*. This is why *niyyah* for fasting is to worship Allah by abstaining from fast-breakers from the break of dawn to sunset.

The act of abstinence is not meant to starve you; it is an act of worship, like Salaat. It is the lack of intention that makes ones acts non-Islamic. Interestingly, you can pursue your regular activities, which have nothing to do with religion, such as maintaining your livelihood and earn a religious reward by the intention. The Prophet (saas) told the believers that by declaring *niyyah*, their relations with their spouses would become charity. The companions asked how would that be a charity *(sadaqah)*? The Prophet responded, "'Don't you know that if he does it in an unlawful way it will be a sin on him?' They said, 'Yes. The same,' he said, 'When he does it in a legal way, it is charity.'" (Muslim)

The evidence for intention, *niyyah*, is mentioned in Al-Qur'an and Sunnah. Allah (SWT) states: "And they have been commanded no more than to worship Allah, offering Him sincere devotion." *(Al-Qur'an, 98:5)*

"They" in this verse refers to the People of the Book, indicating that intention was part of their religious belief, or that they were commanded as the believers were through Prophet Muhammad (saas) to worship Allah sincerely. The structure of this verse is instructive. It did not mention who commanded. Of course, it is Allah. But, you see, this form is used, mentioning Allah indirectly, to indicate that the acts of worship are difficult, and He did not want us to think of them as a burden for the sake of it. He commanded us to fast because he knows we cannot do without these acts of worship.

We see the same use when Allah speaks of fasting: "...Fasting is prescribed to you..." (Al-Quran, 2:183) Also, "the law of equality is prescribed to you." (Al-Quran, 2:178) In both verses, it did not say "who" the subject is. It is not directly mentioned, whereas or when Allah speaks of His *rahman*, mercy, He mentions Himself as if He is informing us that Your Lord has inscribed for Himself mercy. This is like a father or guardian instructing his minor, "You ought to do this and that" instead of telling him "To do this." Or perhaps Allah (SWT) did not mention His name directly to indicate that He (SWT) is not the only One who commands you to worship Him. Your intellect and reasoning also command you to worship your Creator, for He has endowed you with His mercy.

Liya'abudu (to worship) — generally means to humble — but has become a name for every type of worship rendered with humbleness and utmost respect to Allah (SWT). However, the key word is *mukhliseen*, purely intending in their hearts for the pleasure of Allah (SWT) the worship Allah alone. One should declare in his heart that the act he or she is about to undertake is intended for Allah (SWT). It is not for eye service *(riya)*, ear service *(sum'ah)*, saying to be heard, or for any other reasons. The most important thing in Islam is not the quantity of worship *(ebadah)* but the quality. By quality is meant that it is intended for none but Allah. On the other hand, Allah is telling the believer and humanity, you know that I have created everything in creation just for you, that is all of creation. Not half, one-third, one quarter, or a fifth of it, but all of it.

"It is He who has created for you all things that are on earth." *(Al-Qur'an 2:29)* If that is the case, you should not intend with your acts but for Allah alone. Do not intend in your deeds half for Allah and the rest for someone else. You cannot fast three-fourths of a day for Allah and one-fourth for someone else. Nor can you sacrifice two sheep, one for Allah and the other for the ruler. Allah would never accept that. That is the proof of *niyyah* in Al-Qur'an.

In a hadith related by Umar bin Al-Khattab (raa), he said: "I heard the Messenger of Allah (saas), saying: "Deeds are but by intention, and every man shall have all but that which he intended. Thus, he whose migration was for Allah and His Messenger, his migration was for Allah and His Messenger, and he whose migration was to achieve some worldly benefit or to take some woman in marriage, his migration was for that for which he migrated." (Bukhari/Muslim)

This hadith pronounced by the Prophet (saas) explains, in effect, the above verse and attempts to educate the believers before they embark on a course of action. At the outset, as the persecution of the believers reached its peak in Makkah, the Prophet and the believers were ordered to emigrate to Abyssinia, then finally to Madinah, where the Prophet and the believers settled. Migration was, and still is, a sign of faith and a great honor in the sight of Allah. He (SWT) described those men and women who endured that experience as *"Al-Muhajirun,"* declared in Surah 2:218.

"Those who believe and adopted exile and fought (and strove and struggled) in the path of Allah...."

So every person who has an ulterior motive claims he is emigrating to Madinah, to please Allah. But the Prophet (saas) made it clear to the believers that *Hijrah* is not the pain and hardship of traveling and missing the loved ones, but the intent behind it. The hadith defines what constitutes Allah's perception of the deeds of the believer.

Hence, the elements of fasting are two: to worship Allah (SWT) by abstaining from fast-breakers, combined with intention.

THE SEAT OF NIYYAH

There is near consensus among the scholars that the seat of *Niyyah,* or intention, is the heart. What you want to do for what reason and for the sake of whom will be known by none but you and the All Knower, Allah (SWT). Thus, you do not need to utter it with your tongue, "I want to pray, fast, give alms, etc." The exception is on *Hajj,* where verbal utterance of *Talbiyah* is mandated.

In the case of *Sawm* (fasting), You intend in your heart that the abstinence from fast-breakers is meant to be a worship for Allah alone in order to seek His pleasure. If you observe *sahuur* (the last meal before beginning fasting) with this above intent, you will have achieved the requirement of *niyyah*. If you restrain from fast-breakers during daylight hours, with the above intent, you have achieved the requirements of *niyyah*, even if you did not eat *sahuur.*

Hafsah, the Prophet's wife (raa,) related that the Prophet (saas) said: "Whoever does not make *niyyah* (intention for fasting) before dawn, will not have fasted." (Ahmed/Ibn Khzamah)

However, many scholars said this is for obligatory fasting, like Ramadan, but when the fasting is non-essential, one can make *niyyah* during daytime, if he has not eaten anything. The Prophet's wife reported that the Prophet (saas) visited his wives and asked, "'Do you have something to eat?' She said, 'They replied "no." He then said, 'I am fasting.'" (Muslim)

This hadith indicates the believer can have a valid fast, even if he decides after 10:00 a.m. or 4:00 p.m. to hold fast, provided he did not eat or drink anything before the time he makes his decision.

FOR WHOM IS FASTING MANDATORY?

The obligation of fasting is mandatory on a person who has fulfilled these requirements: He or she must be a Muslim, sane, must have reached puberty, must be healthy, and not in a state of travel; and for women, they must be in a state of purity (clean from menstruation and post childbirth bleeding). If a person fulfills the above prerequisites, fasting becomes valid and mandatory. Inferring from this definition, if one of these conditions is missing, the fast will be invalid. Indeed, it may be better to analyze each category of the definition.

Non-Muslim *(Kafir)*

Fasting is not obligatory on a non-Muslim because he is not commanded to fast and even if he decides to fast and follows all the regulations, it will not be accepted by Allah (SWT). If he or she wants to fast the Islamic fast, he has to declare the *Kalimah* first—the declaration of faith—and only then will the fast be accepted. Similarly, the non-Muslim *(Kafir)* is not obligated to perform any Islamic duties. If he converts to Islam during the month of Ramadan, for instance, in the middle of the month, it becomes incumbent upon him to fast the remaining days. There will be no making up the days he missed before becoming Muslim. Allah (SWT) states: "Say to the unbelievers, if they desist from unbelief, their past would be forgiven of them..."
(Al-Qur'an 8:38)

If one converts to Islam during the daytime in Ramadan, say 10:00 a.m. in the morning, he or she should observe the rest of the day in fasting. That is, from 10:00 a.m. until sunset, he should not break his fast.

Insane *(Majnum)*

The insane or mentally retarded person is not obligated to keep his fast because he is deprived of sanity, a key component on which religious duties depend. In a hadith related by Ali Bin Abi Talib (raa), the Messenger of Allah (saas) said: "The Pen that records the deeds has been lifted from three people; the insane person, until he recovers; the sleeping person, until he wakes up; and the minor, until he dreams (i.e., has wet dreams.)" (Ahmed)

This hadith indicates the fast of the insane person, for instance, is not valid because he cannot comprehend the worship, and he cannot meaningfully declare intention *(niyyah)*, without which the acts are invalid. If he has mental relapses whereby he is healthy, and then on occasion is sick, the fast is mandatory upon him during the days and times he is healthy but not when he is unhealthy.

If he intends to fast in the morning, and he falls ill during this time, his fast is good as if he fainted as a result of illness, because he knows that he may experience an attack at certain times. If he gets well during the daytime in Ramadan, he should observe the fast the rest of the day because he is obligated to fast. However, he does not have to make up the day because his case is like that of an unbeliever who becomes a Muslim during daytime or a minor who reached puberty during the day.

Minor *(Sabiyy)*

Similarly, the minor person is not obligated to observe fast *(Sawm)*, because of the previous hadith related by Ali bin Abi Talib, "...And the minor until he dreams." However, it is imperative that the parents or the guardians of the juveniles or adolescents encourage and urge them to fast so they will get used to it. It will be vital training for them in their worship, because they will not have any chance for training as soon as they reach puberty.

In a hadith reported by Rubayyiah Bint Mau'awwidh (raa), the Prophet (saas) sent a messenger to the village of Ansar on the morning of Ashura to inform them: "Whoever wakes in fasting should continue his fasting, whoever wakes up without fasting should complete his day in fasting. So we used to fast, let our young children fast, and go to the Masjid with them. When one of the children cried for food, we would make toys from wool and give them to the children until it was time to break the fast." (Bukhari and Muslim)

This hadith indicates that training minor boys and girls is highly recommended early in life, from about seven years of age for the spiritual, educational, and cultural upbringing of Muslim youth. It is the most powerful symbol of our religion.

PUBERTY—BOYS

Puberty is known in Islamic law as *al-bulugh*, or *Tamyeez*, (coming of age as a man and woman). There are three signs of puberty *(bulugh)*:

1. Discharging semen as a result of wet dreams, known as *inzaalul-manyyi*. Allah (SWT) states: "But when the children among you come of age, let them also ask for permission, as do those senior to them in age..." *(Al-Qur'an, 24–59)*
   In a hadith, the Messenger of Allah (saas) said: "Friday bath *(ghuslul-Jum'ah)* is mandatory upon anyone who has experienced a wet dream." (Bukhari/Muslim) The point in this hadith is that Islamic obligations are not incumbent on anyone until they reach the age of *bulugh*.

2. Appearance of hair around the pubic area is another sign of puberty. If a person sees that even without wet dreams, he

or she has attained puberty. This may happen at the age of thirteen or fourteen, and parents should inform girls and boys about these signs.

3. Reaching 15 years of age: When the person reaches 15, he or she is a man or a woman, and anything that is obligatory on a man or woman is obligatory on him or her from that time on.

In a hadith reported by Abdullah Bin Umar (raa), he said: "My parents brought me to the Messenger of Allah on the eve of the *Uhud* Campaign and I was fourteen years old, so the Prophet (saas) did not enlist me in fighting. But a year later in the Campaign of Al-Khandaqq, I was fifteen, so this time the Prophet (saas) enlisted me in combat." (Muslim) This hadith indicates that the age of 15 is the legal age for a Muslim boy or girl to be responsible for his or her religion as well as worldly responsibilities. Some of us who reside in the western world, seem to think adulthood depends on State laws. In some states it is 18, while in others it is 19, or 21, and so on. This is a very serious mistake, as the juvenile will reach puberty *(bulugh)* and adulthood, but go on without observing his or her Islamic duties, such as Salat, fasting, or being restrained from that which is prohibited.

PUBERTY—GIRLS

Girls reach puberty and adulthood when they experience the above three signs. However, they have a fourth sign, that is, menstruation *(hayd)*. Whenever a girl experiences it, she is a woman even if she is 12 years old. At that time, the *Qalam,* the pen of responsibilities, begins to flow and to record the deeds of the servant, good or bad. It is interesting that in the western world the case is the reverse. You see, when a juvenile reaches the age of puberty in Al-Islam he or she should be careful about anything he or she does or says. On the contrary, in the West when the person comes of age, he or she is allowed to do things which are detrimental to his or her well being. They are licensed to read, watch, and listen to so-called adult material, as if when one is an adult it is time to be irresponsible.

Indeed, if puberty is attained during the days of Ramadan, say at midday, and the young person is fasting, he or she should continue his or her fasting and there will be no obligation on him or her to make up the fast. If he was not fasting, it is incumbent upon him to observe the rest of the day in fasting, because he has become an adult upon whom lslamic rites are obligatory. Girls in menstruation can't observe half day, nor should they make that half day up.

THE ELDERLY (*AL-HARIM*)

When we speak of the elderly people, we are speaking of two categories: the old person who has reached the point of absent-mindedness and aimless talk, (*al-hazyaan*) and the person who cannot comprehend what he or she is doing or saying. There will be no fast for these people, nor will they be required to feed the needy for the days missed, because their case is like that of a child before reaching the age of discretion, *tamyeez*. But if he or she suffers relapses, the fast is mandatory on him, while he comprehends and when he does not comprehend there will be no fast. These rules about the elderly people apply to the rest of their Islamic obligations, including Salaat, Hajj, etc.

PHYSICAL DISABILITY (*AL-'AJIZ*)

The aim of this religion is not to burden people to a point that they will be incapable physically of carrying out the duties mandated by Allah (SWT). This is why when there is clear evidence that fasting will result in the opposite of the intended result, namely endangering the sanctity of life itself, the Lawgiver (*Shaari'e*), makes room for the believer. By physical disability ('al-'ajis), we mean the old person who is mentally sound but physically weak, and observation of the fast would further weaken his body. Also, at this point the fast is not mandatory upon the old person because he is unable to do so. In the case of the terminally ill, like the cancer or AIDS patient whose fasting may worsen their condition, Allah (SWT) states:

"...So fear Allah as much as you can" (*Al-Qur'an 64:16*) Also, "On no soul does Allah place a burden greater than it can bear..." (*Al-Qur'an 2:286*). These two verses indicate that when the body is no longer capable of executing the prescribed duties, the pen that records the deeds ceases to record. These people who have been allowed to break their fast of Ramadan, would have to compensate for each and every day that they break by feeding one indigent person.

Before the fasting of Ramadan was prescribed to the believers, everyone was given a choice between fasting or feeding. This is what Al-Qur'an refers to in chapter "Al-Baqarah":

"...for those who can do it (with hardship) is a ransom, the feeding of the indigent..." (Al-Qur'an 2:184). This verse was abrogated by the verse of Ramadan.

When a believer is incapable of fasting due to the reasons mentioned above, feeding becomes a substitute.

FEEDING (ITAAM)

For feeding, you have a choice between providing a poor person about one kilo and ten grams of wheat, rice, or any kind of staple of the best kind, or to provide a meal after the month of Ramadan, by preparing food and inviting poor people, their number equal to the number of days you missed. Or the whole amount may be given to one to two families. Imam Bukhari (raa) reported that Anas bin Malik, at an advanced age fed poor people bread and meat one or two days every year.

PREGNANT AND NURSING MOTHERS

When a pregnant woman or nursing mother eats, they do so for the health of themselves and their babies. Their decision to fast depends on how they feel. If they feel that fasting may jeopardize their life and injure the unborn or newly born, the Lawgiver gives them permission to break fast. They will have to make it up at any time after Ramadan before the next Ramadan.

TRAVELER

The traveler has a choice between fasting and breaking the fast, regardless of the length of the journey: whether the journey is an emergency, for Hajj, to visit relatives, for business, or if he, the believer, is a frequent traveler like airplane pilots, bus and truck drivers, train engineers, or ship captains. As for cab drivers, if the weather is hot, they may change their working hours to nighttime until the weather is cooler; they would not be considered travelers, and thus break fast. There is one condition for the traveler: that they are not intending with their journey as a masquerade and trick to avoid fasting. If that is the intent, breaking the fast is prohibited and fasting becomes mandatory upon him during the course of the journey.

Allah (SWT) states: "But if any one is ill or on a journey (the prescribed period should be made up) by days later. Allah intends every facility for you; He does not want to put you in difficulties..." *(Al-Qur'an, 2:185)* Allah repeated this verse twice to underscore the fact that it is not abrogated with the general command to fast.

The above verse has considered the hardship encountered on a journey as equal to the hardship in sickness, and thus allows those faced with either condition not to fast. Perhaps the reason can be found in the very meaning of the Arabic word *safar,* which implies exposing oneself during the course of a journey to elements of hardship in transportation, food, time and climate changes, and of cultural shocks of all sorts, or just general wear and tear.

Even in this age of jets and supersonic air travel, traveling poses a danger to the sojourner. Because of this possibility, the Lawgiver has permitted the traveler to eat, so fasting does not add to his already difficult situation. This is why the famous saying goes, "The journey is a type of punishment." He or she, however, would have to make up the day. The permission not to fast during a journey is the same as if a person decides to fast while on a journey, he can do so and the fast is valid.

Type of Journey

The journey that may entail fast-breaking is the one that falls in the category of shortened prayers *(Qasr),* and the period of breakage is the period in which one can shorten the prayer.

What is Better, Fasting or Breaking?

In analyzing the case of the traveler, many scholars said the best in this case is what is easiest for the traveler *(al-ashal),* regarding fasting or not fasting, if they are equal for him, the best thing is to fast, for the following reasons:

This was the preference of the Prophet (saas) as related by Abi Darda (raa), who said: "We journeyed with the Prophet (saas) during Ramadan when it was an extremely hot (season). Some of us shaded ourselves with our hands, because of the extreme heat. No one was fasting among us except the Prophet and Abdullah bin Abi Rawahah. The Prophet broke his fast in consid-

eration for his companions when he knew that the fast was getting the best of the companions and bringing on them an unnec-
essary hardship." (Muslim)

In another hadith reported by Jabir Bin Abdullah (raa): "When
the Prophet (saas) journeyed to Makkah, in the year of victory, he
fasted until he reached a place known as *Kara'ah Al-Ghamin*. He
was informed that the companions who were fasting were having
difficulty with the fast. So, they were waiting to see what he
would do. The Prophet (saas) then requested a goblet full with
water after *Asr* (afternoon) prayer and drank it while everyone
was looking." (Reported by Muslim)

This hadith indicates how fasting is better during a journey,
unless there is unreasonable hardship.

Another reason why fasting is better is because it helps to meet
the obligation of fast without any delay. For you do not know
when death or sickness may come; besides, it is easier to fast
when all the believers are fasting at the same time. This is why
they say that the difficult obligations, when done with other Muslims, become easier. It is easier to fast the whole month of Ramadan; whereas, when a person misses one day of Ramadan, he
may put off redeeming his fast until Sha'aban, one month before
the next Ramadan.

If fasting is difficult for him during the course of a journey, the
traveler should break his fast. In previous hadith reported by Jabir
(raa), when the Prophet broke this fast because of the difficulty of
the believers, he was told that some people insisted on fasting. The
Prophet (saas) said, "they are rebels, they are rebels." (Muslim)

In another hadith by Jabir bin Abdullah (raa) he said: "During
one of the Prophet's journeys, he saw a heavy crowd around a
man who was being shaded. The Prophet (saas) inquired, What
is this? They said He is a faster. 'The Prophet (saas), said: It is not
righteousness to fast during a journey.'" (Muslim/Bukhari)

THE NON-TERMINALLY ILL

When a person becomes ill and his prognosis indicates a serious condition, but not a terminal illness, and the patient is not in
a life-threatening situation, he is granted permission (*rukhsah*) to
break his fast.

This permission does not include simple illnesses, such as a
headache or stomach ache. All these do not warrant breaking the

fast. If fasting becomes harmful for the patient, then it is becomes mandatory for him to break his fast. Allah (SWT) said: "Nor kill (or destroy) yourselves, for Allah has been to you Most Merciful." *(Al-Qur'an, 4:29)* Elsewhere, He stated: "And make not your own hands contribute to (your) destruction..." *(Al-Qur'an, 2:195)*

These two verses are general in everything that one may do which might undermine the integrity of life. In a Hadith reported by Bukhari, the Messenger of Allah (SWT) said: "Your soul, indeed, has rights on you!" (Bukhari) Among its rights is you protecting it from harm.

If one falls sick during the daytime and completing fast becomes hard on him, he is permitted to break his fast for this reason. If he is cured during the daytime, say 10:00 a.m., and he has not been fasting, his fast for that day is not valid because he was not fasting at the beginning of the day, and the fast is for all day not half of the day.

However, he would have to make up the day or days he missed after Ramadan. Allah (SWT) states: "...Fasting is for a fixed number of days, but if any of you is ill, or on a journey, the prescribed number (missed) should be made up..." *(Al-Qur'an, 2:184)*

This verse indicates that when the believer intends to fast and discovers during a journey that he or she can not continue, he should break it and make it up later. If a traveler who is not fasting returns home during the daytime, his fasting of that day is invalid because he did not observe it from the beginning of the day. The mandatory fast starts with the break of dawn.

Should he observe the rest of the day in fasting or not? Some scholars say he should restrain from eating the rest of the day as respect for the fast, although he would have to make it up later. But others said there is no valid reason to force a person who has been permitted by the Lawgiver not to fast at the beginning of the day, to abstain for the rest of the day.

That is why Abdullah bin Mas'eud (raa) said, "Whoever eats in the beginning of the day should eat at the end of the day." (Majalis Shar Ramadan) This means if a person is allowed to eat in the early part of the morning due to certain valid reasons, it is lawful for him to eat at the later part of the day. This is also the ruling of Imams Malik and Shafi'e. But they say he should not eat or drink in public because no one knows the reason of his breaking and, they may think badly of him, or some weak-minded person may try to emulate his action.

BREAKING FAST TO SAVE LIFE

Whoever is compelled to break his fast for a valid reason, such as donating blood to save a life, and he or she does not have strength to do so without food, the person is allowed to break his fast. Indeed, it is mandatory on him to break, because saving a life is mandatory. As they say: *Mala, yatimul wajib illa bihi fahuwa wajid.* (An action necessary to accomplish a mandatory act is mandatory.) Similarly, the person who needs to break his fast to gain strength so as to participate in defending Muslim life and property should break his fast.

In a hadith reported by Abi Sa'ed Al-Khudri (raa) he said: "We journeyed with the Messenger of Allah to Makkah while observing the fast of Ramadan. When we stopped at a place, he said, 'You are getting near your enemy and breaking fast will help you gain your strength.' This was a concession. Some of us continued to fast, while others broke their fast. Then, we stopped again, and the Messenger of Allah (saas) said, 'You are meeting your enemy in the morning and breaking fast is better for your stamina. Break!' That was an order. So, we broke.'" (Muslim/Ahmed) This hadith indicates how the desire to regain strength is an independent reason, besides a journey, to permit someone to break his fast.

REDEMPTION OF RAMADAN *(AL-QADA)*

The groups who are permitted to break fast due to the reasons mentioned should redeem the day(s) they missed after Ramadan. Allah (SWT) states: "The prescribed number (should be made up) from days later." *(Al-Qur'an 2:185)* If he breaks the whole month, the whole month should be redeemed. If the month is 30 days, 30 days are due on him. If the month is 29 days, 29 days are due.

Technically, the time period of redemption is the whole year before next Ramadan. If he missed ten days, the redemption is due ten days before next Ramadan. However, it is preferred to redeem as soon as the obstacle is removed, because it is better to meet the obligation and free yourself from the responsibility without delay, this is known as *(Ibraudh-Dhimmah)*

It should not be delayed until next Ramadan without any good reason. The Prophet's wife Aishah has been reported as saying, "Sometime when I miss some days of Ramadan, I would not be able to redeem them except in the month of Shaaban." The narrator of the Hadith, Yahaya, added: "She was busy serving the Messenger of Allah (saas)." (Bukhari and Muslim). Delaying to the next Ramadan may lead to piling up fasts which may be difficult for him to make up, or he may die in the mean time. If he died before making it up, there will be no blame on him because Allah gave him allowance to make up missed fasts. But if he is able but neglected it, his next of kin should redeem on his behalf.

The Prophet (saas) said: "Whoever dies before redeeming his missed fast, his next of kin should redeem it for him." (Bukhari/Muslim) Indeed, a group of relatives can redeem it for him, each fasting a certain amount of days until the *qada* is complete. If there is no next of kin, or there is one who does not wish to fast on his behalf, his guardian *(Wali)* can redeem it by feeding people instead of fasting.

The proof for this case is two things: analogy *(al-Qiyaas)* and Sunnah. The fear of the elderly person fasting, in that it may endanger his life, is similar to the case of pregnant and nursing women. Some said the same text cited as a proof for permitting the elderly to break fast and feed poor people can be cited here too, because the verse is general.

In a Hadith reported by Anas Bin Malik Alkaaby (raa), the Messenger of Allah (saas) said: "Allah permitted the sojourner to break fast (and make it up), and his Salat is cut in half. Also, pregnant women and nursing mothers are permitted to break their fast." (Tirmidhi)

If menstruation appears while the woman is fasting, even if it is seconds before sunset, the fast of that day is invalidated and she should make the day up, that is, if the fast is a mandatory fast, like Ramadan; but if it is a voluntary fast, she has the option of making it up or not. Should menstruation appear during daytime, the rest of the day's fast is invalidated.

If menstruation ceases during the night, even seconds before *Fajr*, the fast of that day becomes mandatory, because she is among the eligible, and the obstacle *(mawaani'e)* to eligibility has been removed. She should fast even before she takes *ghusl* (shower, or purifying bath).

Similarly, with a woman bleeding as a result of childbirth *(nifaas)*, her case is identical to that of a menstruating woman.

DAYS IN WHICH FASTING IS PROHIBITED

As much as fasting is one of the most important pillars of Al-Islam, there are certain days during which the Lawgiver prohibited the believer to fast.

1. The two 'Eids

There are two annual celebrations in Islam: *'Eidul Fitr* and *'Eidul Adha*. These *'Eids* symbolize the period of happiness when Muslims all over the world commemorate the festivities with the praise of Allah and public prayers after which they go home to feast with family and friends. Obviously, fasting and the Eid do not mix. If it is Eidul-Fitr, the fast-breaking feast, how could one celebrate the ending of the annual fast period with a fast? And if it is Eidul Adha, Festivity of Sacrifice, how could one sacrifice an animal and not eat it?

This is why the majority of Muslims agreed that fasting on the days of Eid is prohibited. If you have to make up a fast, it should not be on these days. In a hadith related by Umar bin Al-Khattab (raa), he said: "The Messenger of Allah (saas) prohibited fasting on these two days: on the day of fast-breaking, because you have just broken your fast of Ramadan and on the day of sacrifice you are supposed to eat from your sacrifice." (Ahmed and others)

2. Three Days Following *'Eidul Adha*, The Days of *Tashreeq*.

The days of *Tashreeq* are the three days following *Eidul Adha*. These three days are the most important days as far as the festivity of Eid and public display of happiness are concerned. Muslims usually take off work and visit other Muslims to share this happiness with them. These are the days of giving gifts to the family, relatives, and the needy.

Abu Hurairah (raa) reported the Prophet (saas) sent Abdullah bin Huzaifah (raa) to go around *Mina* to announce to the pilgrims, "Do not fast these days (three days after 'Arafah). These are days of eating and drinking and remembrance of Allah (SWT)." (Ahmed).

Although the hadith addressed the congregation of pilgrims, it's meaning and implication are general to every Muslim who is being advised not to observe fast on these days. This is the understanding of the majority of scholars. The minority said if one vowed to expiate, or make up his fast, he may fast during these days. The majority responded that the minority opinion is good but it has no proof contrary to the one mentioned above that it would be okay to fast during these days.

3. Singling Out Friday for Fasting

Friday, *Jum'ah*, is a weekly festival for Muslims. They celebrate with congregational prayer and meeting each other. The Lawgiver, *(Shaare'e)* prohibited singling it out with the observance of fast. This is why the scholars said: This is an exception or undesired prohibition, *Makruuh*, not of the same strength as the absolute prohibition of *Haram*; that is, one can observe it, provided that the Friday fast is cushioned by fasting the day before and the day after, or that Friday occurs on the day of 'Arafah, or on the tenth of Muharram, as these are days their fasting is highly encouraged.

The prohibition here rests on the hadith related by Abdullah Ibn 'Umar (raa), who said: "The Prophet (saas) visited his wife Juwayrah bint Harith and found her fasting on Friday." He asked her, 'Did you fast yesterday? No,' she replied. He asked again: 'Do you plan to fast tomorrow?' she replied, 'No.' He said: 'Then, break your fast.'" (Ahmed)

In another hadith reported by 'Amir Al-Ashairee (raa): I heard the Prophet say Friday is your day of feast, so do not observe it in fasting unless you fast a day before and a day after.' Jabir bin Abdullah (raa) related: The Prophet (saas) said: "Do not single out *Jum'ah* night among the nights for nightly prayer *(Tahajjud)*, nor single out Friday for fasting unless it happens to coincide with fasting that you are accustomed to." (Muslim)

These hadiths are proof that the prohibition is with the condition that a believer has set his mind to fast only Friday. The desire to single out this otherwise important day with undue emphasis is what the Lawgiver wants to prevent. A Muslim does not live only for *Jum'ah*. One can see that in other religions, only certain days are accorded any religious significance while the rest of the days are relegated for secular pursuits.

4. Singling Out Saturday for Fast

For the very reason why we are forbidden to single out Friday for fasting, we are also prohibited to fast only on Saturdays or, in that case, only on Sundays. But there is also another reason. Saturday is the weekly festival for the Jews as Sunday is for the

Christians. Islam has encouraged and instructed the believers to stay away and not lend any religious significance to these two days. We do not fast on our day of feast. We can fast on the day of their feast but without singling it out. This is why the statement prohibiting the customs of Saturday fasting is very strong. The Prophet (saas) said: "Do not fast on Saturday, unless it is part of what Allah has prescribed for you. If you could not find anything to eat but a grape skin or a piece of wood, you should chew it." (Ahmed) The Prophet's wife Umm Salmah (raa) stated: "The Prophet used to observe Saturday and Sunday with fasting (along with other days), and would say, These are the *Eids* of polytheists and I like to differ with them." This hadith implies that a believer should not lend spiritual significance to the religious festivities of non-Muslims.

5. No Fasting on the Day of Doubt *(Yamush-Shakk)*

I mentioned earlier that intention (niyyah), is one of the two important elements of fasting. It implies certainty or an effort to ascertain the day of fast. There is no such thing as saying that I will fast if it happens to be Ramadan. That shaky assumption is not accepted in starting the Fast, and it is known as *sawm yawmush-shakk*. In a *athar* reported from Amaar bin Yaasir (raa) he said: "Whoever fasts the day he is doubtful (weather it is the first day or not or the last day of Ramadan or not), he has disobeyed the Messenger of Allah (Aba Qasim)." (Tirmidhi)

Fasting in this manner, even if the day is correct, is not valid. Abu-Harairah reported that the Messenger of Allah (saas) said: "Do not fast a day or two before Ramadan, unless that fast coincides with a fast the person usually observes. In that case, he may fast that day" (Muslim/ Bukhari)

On the authority of this hadith, many scholars forbid a man or woman to decide in doubt. No matter what the outcome is, that day would have to be redeemed.

6. No Fasting for Life *(Sawmud-Dahr)*

The essence of Islam and its noble teachings always take into account the general interests and welfare, *al-maslahah*, of Muslims. Thus, the prohibition of fasting for a whole year or for life, for the simple reason that it may lead to one's physical ruin or religious asceticism. Both are vehemently rejected by Islam; and to relegate Islam to such ascetic, rigid abstinence would undoubt-

edly infringe on the believer's other religious and social obligations. The Messenger of Allah (saas) has been reported as saying:
"No fast for whoever fasts forever." (Muslim and Bukhari)

Inferring from this hadith, the scholars say that if the fast is
interrupted during the days of the Eids and three days following
them there is no prohibition. They cited another Hadith in which
the Prophet (saas) advised Hamzah Al Aslami (raa) to continue
his fast, when he said to him: "Fast, if you so desire, and break."
The preference for anyone who would like to fast that much is to
fast the fast of Prophet David, who has been reported as fasting
one day and breaking the next.

7. No Married Woman Should Fast without the Consent of her Husband

If a wife decides to fast a voluntary fast, it is incumbent upon
her to inform her husband and seek his permission, because he
may be desiring her during her fast and cannot fulfil his desire,
because she is fasting. In addition, he may be tempted to commit
a sin. This prohibition rests on the hadith reported by Abu
Hurairah (raa) that the Prophet (saas) said: "Women should not
fast one day while her husband is present, without his permission, except in Ramadan." (Muslim, Bukhari and others)

Deducing from this hadith, if the husband travels or he is
absent, she may fast, or if he is sick or he is unable to consum-
mate there is no need to seek his permission.

8. Continuous Fast of Days and Nights without Break is Prohibited *(Wisaal)*

Wisaal is to fast days and nights non-stop, without break, and
continuing yet with another day and night and so on. This kind
of fasting is prohibited. In a hadith reported by the Messenger of
Allah (saas), he said: "Beware of *wisaal*, fasting nights and days
uninterrupted." He repeated the warning three times. When the
companions inquired, 'O Messenger of Allah, don't you practice
Wisal sometimes?' The Prophet (saas) explained, 'That is true but
you are not like me. My Lord nourishes me with food and drink.
So, observe of the deeds what you are capable of.'" (Bukhari/
Muslim)

However, the Islamic jurists, while analyzing the whole case of
wisaal, concluded that the restriction may be lifted if the fast is
broken by the time of the last meal, *sahuur*. In a Hadith related by

Abi Sa'eed Al-Khudari, the Messenger of Allah (saas) said: "Do not practice *wisaal*, however, whoever wants to continue, may do so up to the time of the last meal, *sahuur*, and then eat." (Bukhari)

VOLUNTARY FAST *(TATAWWA'U)*

It has been mentioned earlier that there are two kinds of fasting, obligatory *(Fard)* and voluntary *(Tatawwu'u)*. The first has been discussed in some detail. Now we will discuss voluntary fast.

In Islam, deeds do not end with nor rest only on the obligatory deeds. *Fard* are the minimum duties required on an average believer. Thus, the Lawgiver instituted voluntary deeds, to assist a devoted believer who has the will to do more, and also assist the believers in general in repairing and complimenting their obligatory deeds with voluntary deeds. The voluntary deed comes with every pillar in Islam, including fasting.

The voluntary fast is for men as well as for women. The method and restriction of this fast is no different from regular Ramadan fast. The difference is in the *niyyah* (intention).

FASTING SIX DAYS OF *SHAWWAL* (*SITTU MIN SHAWWAL*)

Shawwal is the tenth month in the lunar calendar, as mentioned earlier. The first of *Shawwal* is *Eidul Fitr*. After the festivity of Eid it is recommended to observe six days of fast. This fast may be observed continuously non-break, or it may be observed one day at a time. If you observe it continuously, you may start on the fourth day and end on the ninth day of *Shawwal*, or you may select days at random, provided you complete six days before the end of *Shawwal*. For instance, you may observe the third, fifth, seventh, ninth, 14th and 15th days. Abu Ayyub Al-Ansari (raa) related that the Messenger of Allah, (saas), said:

"Whoever observes the Ramadan fast and follows it with six days of fast in Shawwal, it is as if he has fasted *Dahr* (the whole year)." (Bukhari) It has been mentioned earlier that *Dahr* means the whole year. Possibly it may also mean forever, or for life.

Analyzing this hadith, our jurists *(Ulama)* explained how according to this hadith, a Muslim who fasts during Ramadan every year and follows it with six days fast of Shawwal, will be credited for fasting a whole lifetime. The Jurists correctly said: a good deed (hasanah) is rewarded a minimum of ten times its equivalent. It follows, then, that one Ramadan is equivalent to ten months of fasting, and the clincher, six days, is equal to two months, $(6 \times 10 = 60)$. That undoubtedly completes the year's twelve months. Thus, we see the wisdom and the reason behind the Prophet's (saas) mentioning of six days of fasting after Ramadan in *Shawwal*, not five or seven.

FASTING ON THE DAY OF *ARAFAH*

The ninth day of *Zulhijjah* is the day of 'Arafah. It is the day when pilgrims stand on the plain of *'Arafah* to pray. On this day, Muslims all over the world who do not witness the annual *Hajj*, should spend the day in fasting in preparation for the three days festivity following *Eidul Adha*.

Abu Hafasah (raa) said the Prophet (saas) said: "Fasting on the day of *'Arafah* absolves the sins for two years: the previous year and the coming years, and fasting on 'Ashura, (the tenth day) of Muharram atones for the sins of previous years." (Reported by Jama'ah except Bukhari and Tirmidhi)

In another hadith, the Prophet's wife Hafsah (raa) said: "Four things the Messenger of Allah never neglected: Observing fast on the day of *'Ashura*, (on the tenth of Muharam), three days every month, and offering *Fajr* sunnah prayers early in the morning." (Muslim)

These ahadiths are proof that fasting on the tenth of *Zulhijjah*, the day before *Eidul Adha* was a lifelong practice of the Prophet (saas) as his wife reported.

There are some reports that fasting is prohibited on the day of *'Arafah*. However, it must be understood that this refers to a person performing Hajj. If a person is on Hajj, there is no fast for him or her on the day of *'Arafah*. That is undoubtedly a blessing for him because of the hardships of the pilgrimage. In a hadith reported by Umm al-Fadl (raa) she said: "The companions doubted whether the Prophet was fasting on 'Arafah or not. She decided to prove to them that he was not, so she said, 'I sent to him milk, which he drank while he was delivering the *Khutbah* on *'Arafah.*'" (Bukhari)

Prohibiting the pilgrim from fasting on these days is a great mercy for him, for fasting will exert undue hardship on the person performing the Hajj, while he is concerned with his pilgrimage. Above all, the pilgrim would not be fasting anyway because he is traveling.

FASTING IN *MUHARRAM*
(The First Month of Islamic Year)

Fasting in the month of Muharram is highly desired, especially on the tenth day, *Ashura*. The Messenger of Allah (saas) has been reported as saying when asked which prayer is better after obligatory prayer: "Prayer in the middle of the night." He was asked again which fast is better after Ramadan. He said: "In the month that is called *Al-Muharam.*" (Ahmed, Muslim, and Abu Dawud)

This hadith clearly indicates the importance of voluntary fasting in Muharram, among all the months. The Prophet (saas) however, emphasizes the fast of the tenth day, *Ashura*. The word *"Ashura"* is derived from *Ashara*, which means ten. The observation of this day goes back to Prophet Musa bin 'Emran (saas). In a hadith related by Ibn Abbas (raa) when the Messenger of Allah (saas) came to Medina, he found the Jews fasting the day of *Ashura*. He inquired why do they did so. They replied that it was a good day, the day which Allah delivered Prophet Musa (saas) and the children of Israel from their enemy. As gratitude Musa (saas) fasted that day.

The Prophet (saas) responded: "I have more right to Musa than you. He fasted the day and commanded the believers to fast." (Agreed upon.)

This hadith indicates that the Prophet (saas) was in complete agreement with Prophet Musa (saas) as well as the other prophets. The point here is that the Messenger of Allah would always do an act of worship if it was prophecy reported from any of the prophets. Earlier, we see how he told us that the best voluntary fast is the fast of Dawud.

This is why the following hadith is of great interest to us. Ibn Abbas related when Prophet Muhammad (saas) observed the day of *Ashura* and commanded his followers to observe it, they asked him: "O Messenger of Allah (saas) this is the day the Jews, and Christians respect and honor..." The Prophet (saas) promised them that "Next year Allah willing, we shall fast the ninth, *tasuu'aa*, along with the tenth." By the next Muharram, the Prophet (saas) had already passed away. Because of the believers, desire to emulate Prophet Musa in fasting on *Ashura* and to not have the desire to participate in the festivity of the People of the Book, who have reduced the day to a mere formality. The Prophet (saas) decided to remove this ambiguity with the fast of the ninth day.

Our 'Ulama, analyzing all reports from the Prophet (saas) regarding Muharram, stated the fast of Muharram can be viewed in three ways:

1. Fasting three days of Muharram, the ninth, tenth and eleventh.
2. Fasting on the ninth and tenth days because of two previous Hadiths.
3. Fasting on the tenth day alone.

It is to celebrate on the day of *Ashura*. In a hadith by Jabir Bin Abdullah, the Messenger of Allah (saas) said: "Whoever spends generously on himself and his family on the day of *Ashura*, Allah will provide for him generously the rest of his year." (Al-Bayhaqi)

FASTING OF *SHA'ABAN*

It is recommended to fast most of the eighth month Sha'aban. However, there is no proof or merit to the fasting half of Sha'aban *(nisf Sha'aban)*, as is commonly known, because there is no verifiable evidence *(daleel)* to support that fasting. 'Aisha (raa) related: "I have never seen the Prophet (saas) complete the fasting of a month at all, except the month of Ramadan. I have never seen him fast most of a month, except Sha'aban." (Bukhari/Muslim)

The hadith indicates clearly the Prophet's Sunnah in preparation for the month of Ramadan is fasting most of the eighth month, Sha'aban, in anticipation for Ramadan. Thus, the believer may fast during Sha'aban as much as he or she pleases, the more the better.

Again, there is no evidence, or at least the hadith is incorrect, that Sha'aban is the month in which the annual recording of deeds is done. The hadith in question is reported by Osamah Bin Zaid (raa) who asked the Prophet (saas): "O Messenger of Allah, why don't you observe fast in other months as you do in Sha'aban?" The Messenger responded: "This is a month most people neglect, between Rajab and Ramadan, the month in which (the annual deeds of humanity) are raised to the Lord of the worlds. So, I want my deeds to be raised while I am observing fast" (Abu Dawud, Nasa'e, and Ibn Khuzaimah) This Hadith is not authentic, for it contradicts a verse in Al-Qur'an, according to many scholars. They stated Allah (SWT) said: "We sent it down during a blessed night, for We (ever) wish to warn against evil. In that night is made distinct every affair of wisdom." *(Al-Qur'an, 44–3)*

This is the Night of Power *(Lailatul Qadr)*, the night in which the deeds of humanity are returned and the decrees for the following year are announced to the angels, not as the above hadith alleged. The Qur'anic commentators said: On this night, Allah will decree and explain what will take place in the affairs of humanity and the world, their earnings, longevity, who will live or die, what type of deeds, good or bad, virtues or non-virtues and what type of work. Allah (SWT) will reveal from the protective slate, *Lawhul-Mahfuz)* the record of every living being to the Angels as the annual records are being raised and stored away.

FASTING ON MONDAY AND THURSDAY

It has been reported that the Messenger of Allah (saas) fasted the second and fifth days of the week, namely, Monday and Thursday. These two days, as the Hadith explained, are the days in which, twice weekly, the deeds are raised into the heavens and are the days of forgiveness. Abu Hurairah related the Messenger of Allah (saas) was asked why he rarely missed these two days of fasting. He replied: "Indeed, the deeds of humanity are exhibited every Monday and Thursday. Then Allah will further pardon every Muslim for every behavior, except the two believers who part from each other's company; Allah will say to the angels delay the two of them." (Ahmed)

He (saas) was asked again. He said, "I observe this day (Monday) in fasting because it was a day in which I was born, and on it the revelation of (Al-Qur'an) was inaugurated." (Muslim)

This hadith added another reason for fasting on Monday. It was the Messenger's birthday. This is an indication of the fallacy of the annual celebration of the Prophets birthday, which some Muslims observe every year on the 12th of Rabeeual Awwal. This is nothing but innovation, because there is no record of a hadith regarding it. The only thing reported in respect to the birth of Muhammad (saas) is this hadith, and that is celebrated with fasting on Mondays.

One may ask also why is his birth celebrated? Undoubtedly, the birth of the Seal of the Prophets represents a mercy to humanity, as it marked the dawning of a new era in human history.

The inauguration of the Book of Allah, Al-Qur'an, which confirmed and updated previous scriptures occurred on a Monday, when Allah (SWT) revealed the first *ayah* of Al-Qur'an in the cave of *Hira*. That was an important event because that was the time humanity began receiving the correct updated manual of life.

For a believer who seeks nearness to Allah (SWT) fasting, as mentioned earlier, is an important and proper way to offer worship (Ebadah). Abu Az-Zarr Al-Ghifari (raa) reported that: "The Messenger of Allah (saas) commanded us to fast in every calendar month three days: the thirteenth, fourteenth and fifteenth. The Prophet added fasting these days is like fasting a whole year." (Nasa'e)

There is room in the way these days are observed, because there are other Ahadiths relating to the Sunnah of three days fasting that can be observed in a different way. The report indicated that the Prophet (saas) fasted every month on Saturday, Sunday and Monday. In different months, he would fast Tuesday, Wednesday and Thursday. Elsewhere, he was observed fasting on the first Thursday of the month, and the following Monday, and the following Monday. Of these methods, any one you choose is proper and correct.

FASTING AND BREAKING FAST

Some devoted believers may wish to fast forever, oblivious to hardship in their life, not to mention the fact that this type of fasting is not in harmony with the spirit of Al-Islam. When reports of Abdullah Bin Amru's continuous fasting reached the Messenger of Allah (saas), Abdullah related later:

"'The Messenger told me, I have been informed that you observe night prayer and a daily fast. Ibn 'Amru answered, 'Yes!' O Messenger of Allah. The Messenger advised, him: 'Fast a day and break a day. Pray at night and sleep. For your body has rights over you, your wife has rights over you, and your guest has rights over you. Indeed, it will perfectly suffice you to fast three days in every month.' 'Amru strongly pointed out that he was capable of observing the fast in the fashion he was doing. But the Messenger advised against it. Ibn 'Amru said, 'Then I explained to him that I have the strength to do it.' The Messenger of Allah (saas) then said: 'Observe three days fasting starting from Friday (and then break).' Ibn 'Amru said: 'I strongly stressed to him that I could, and he vigorously said I should not.' The Messenger of Allah then instructed, 'Observe your fast as the Prophet of Allah, Dawud, (David, saas), used to observe and do not exceed it.'

'How did he fast?' 'Amru asked. The Prophet (saas) said: 'Prophet Dawud (saas) used to fast a day and break the next.'" (Ahmad)

This hadith is instructing and revealing that the objectives in the command to fast are not to unduly injure, or deny the body the natural way of living. It also indicates the caring side of this Messenger of mercy as he tried to convince Amru that his decision to spend the rest of his life in fasting was not in harmony with Islam. With continuous fasts one loses the physical and spiritual benefits. Physically, because it becomes a routine and the body loses the benefits of the way the fast is structured. Spiritually, one feels the numbness, and boredom of the heart. The spouses' right to marital association is denied as the continuous fasting decreases the sexual desire.

The soul is affected only by what intrudes upon it, not by what it is accustomed to. Do you not see that the doctors will advise a person not to take a drug, as a matter of routine, unless the body needs it, lest the same drug will be ineffective when the person gets sick.

The hadith indicates that no one has the right to use his or her body exclusively in the way they desire. In every undertaking, one should bear in mind the other legal rights. The responsibilities of a person are multiple. For while you may think you are worshipping Allah, you may well be violating Allah's rules, because you lose the balance in worship by infringing on the rights of your body when you overly deny it the element of survival.

If you fail to fulfill the marital covenant towards your wife or husband, you may be making her or him vulnerable and susceptible to unlawful, immoral acts. The Hadith also reveals and indicates the beautiful relationship between the teacher and the student, and how the Messenger was very patient with a companion who had unlimited energy, and did not mind spending it in fasting. It reveals how the Prophet (saas) encouraged the believers to express their opinions and ask questions while observing the etiquette of respect to the Messenger of Allah (saas) who said: "The best (voluntary fast in the sight of Allah) is the fast of Prophet Dawud, and the best nightly voluntary prayer is the prayer of Prophet Dawud." The Messenger explained, "He used to sleep half of the night then pray one-third of the night, then sleep one sixth of the night. In fasting, he used to fast a day and break the next." (Ahmed)

It is a mercy from Allah (SWT) that our Prophet Muhammad (saas) is in tune with all the previous revelations' as we see in Al-Qur'an and the Sunnah. It is rich spiritual information made available through him (saas) to this Ummah.

PERMISSION REGARDING VOLUNTARY FAST

The observer of voluntary fasting is his own leader. That is why he is permitted, if he so desires, to abort the fast. This is the verdict of many scholars relying on the evidence of the following citations.

Umm Hanee (raa) related that, "The Messenger of Allah entered into my quarters the day that Makkah was conquered. He was offered water to drink. He drank and passed it to me. I told him I was fasting! The Messenger (saas) instructed. "The observer of a voluntary fast is the leader of his own self. If he wishes, he can continue the fast, and if he wants he can break." (Ahmad)

Elsewhere, Abu Sa'eed Al-Khudri (raa) said, "I invited the Messenger of Allah (saas). He came with his companions. When the food was brought, a man refused to eat. He said, I am fasting.' The Messenger of Allah (saas) commented: Your brother invited you and he has taken the trouble and incurred the cost for your sake. Break your fast and make it up with another day if you want.'" (Bayhaki)

These two ahadiths are evidence that the voluntary fast is different from the mandatory fast in that the observer is allowed with or without a valid reason to abort the obligation of fasting. However, the second report shows also that it is desired to make up the aborted day.

RULES OF FASTING *(ADAABUS SIYAAM)*

In Islam, for any act of worship to be valid and acceptable, it must be observed in accordance with the instruction of Allah (SWT) and the practice of the Messenger of Allah (saas). Obviously, we did not know about the fasting until we were told about it. It would be unwise to just decide to fast in the way one wishes. That is why there are in Islamic Law (Shari'ah) rules of fasting *(Adab As-Siyam)*. Observation of these rules helps the devotee maximize the physical as well as spiritual benefits of fasting.

They are:

SAHUUR

This is a light meal taken shortly before the break of dawn. There is consensus that this meal is a highly recommended Sunnah.

In reports by Bukhari and Muslim, Anas (raa) related that the Messenger of Allah said: "Take your early morning meal for in that is a blessing." In another report by Miqdam bin Ma'a-diyikarib (raa) the Messenger of Allah (saas) said: "Take this early morning meal for it is a blessed meal."

In both ahadiths the statement underscores the importance of *sahuur*, and to caution anyone from thinking they can just stay without a meal all night and continue with fasting. This may explain why the statement came as a command. Although it is not mandatory to eat *sahuur*, it is highly encouraged so that anyone intending to fast will make an effort to take *sahuur*.

The crux of the matter is not to show how strong you are, but how obedient you are. *Sahuur*, above all, ensures that the devotee has the energy he or she will need during the course of the day, and it makes the fast easier.

WHAT CONSTITUTES *SAHUUR*?

Sahuur can be achieved by a large meal, a small meal, or even by a sip of water or soup. In a report by Abu Sa'eed Al-Khudri (raa) the Messenger of Allah (saas) said, "*Sahuur* is a blessed meal, do not neglect it even if it is a mouthful of drink. For Allah and the Angels bless those who observe it." (Ahmed)

You see, what reaches Allah is the intent that you have made a genuine effort to obey Allah in fasting. This is why it is recommended to make intention with the *sahuur*, to emulate the Prophet, and to eat the food to gain strength and energy during fasting, so as to get the reward from Allah. The hadith also contains the information that during the course of this meal the faster receives a special blessing that cannot be found elsewhere: that Allah (SWT) blesses your meal and that the angels seek on your behalf forgiveness for you during *sahuur*. Thus, with *sahuur* you receive both physical and spiritual blessings.

TIME OF *SAHUUR*

The time for sahuur begins from midnight until the break of dawn. It is recommended, however, to delay it till shortly before the time of *Subh* (morning) prayer.

In a hadith by Zaib bin Thabit (raa) he related that: "'We ate *sahuur* with the Messenger of Allah (saas) then we went to pray *Subh*.' I asked the Messenger 'What was the time period between sahuur and prayer?' He responded 'The time period between them is the equivalent of the time it takes to recite fifty verses in Al-Qur'an.'" (Bukhari and Muslim)

This citation is instructive in that it settles the question of whether one should stop eating before morning prayer *(Subh/ Fajr)*, or before sunrise, as we see in certain prayer times tables showing the so-called *shuruq* (the sunrise, which some think is the time to stop eating). The hadith is explicit. The recommendation to delay *Sahuur* is only to the hour or so before *(Subh)*. The mentioning of the period of recitation of fifty verses (ayats) is a cushion or a grace period in which food or drink should not be taken. All the reports that recommend delay of *Sahuur* must be understood in this way.

During the time of the Messenger of Allah (saas), the tradition of two *adhans* (or call to prayer) was established, and it has continued up until now in some Muslim countries. The first *adhan* is to indicate the beginning of *sahuur*: the *adhan* of Abdullah Ibn Umm Maktum (raa). The second is the *adhan* of Bilal Ibn Rabah (raa): the adhan of *Salaah*, a morning prayer.

However, if you hear the second *adhan* while you are eating or drinking, you should immediately stop eating in preparation for fasting.

DOUBTING THE BREAK OF DAWN

Even in the age of watches and alarm clocks, sometimes we doubt whether it is time to stop eating. In this event, one should eat and drink until he is certain and no longer in doubt about the break of dawn. No decision on Islamic deeds should be based on doubt. Allah (SWT) made the determining factor in every affair certainty. He (SWT) says:

"And eat and drink until the white thread of dawn appears to you distinct from it's black thread." *(Al-Quran 2:184)* As I mentioned earlier, by "White thread" is meant the light of the day.

And "black thread" is meant darkness of the night. Hence, the verse is explicit in that eating and drinking are permitted until the doubt and uncertainty are removed from your mind.

A man told Ibn Abbas, (raa), that he observed *Sahuur* and he only stopped when he doubted about the break of dawn. Ibn Abbas (raa) instructed him to eat as long as he doubted until he doubts no more. Similar reports are attributed to many companions and scholars inferring from the above verse.

With the advance in time keeping technology, proliferation of wrist watches, and alarm clocks, the possibility of uncertainty is minimized, at least in the case of a believer who has a time keeping device. These time pieces can be set, not only to sound an alarm, but to call *Al Adhan*, recite some verse, or simply just tell you to get up for *sahuur*.

In the heartland of the Muslim world, the states take the responsibility for public announcements with the firing of cannons, radio, or television announcements. There has evolved a special culture of Ramadan in many countries.

Working hours in some Muslim countries during Ramadan are changed to night, virtually changing or shifting daytime activities to night. In some countries, the governments are not involved in public announcements, but some families and volunteers over the years have taken the duty of wake-up calls by going door to door, in groups and individually in an attempt to wake up the city for Sahuur.

It would be excellent if Muslims in non-Muslim countries try to adjust their working hours and annual vacations during Ramadan, so as to allow themselves the maximum use of the blessed month.

HASTENING TO BREAK FAST

The Lawgiver highly recommended that the fast be broken as soon as the sun set is certain. Although newspapers, in their daily almanac, mention the time of sunset and sunrise, one should be strongly advised to look through the window to make sure the sun has set. For example, you might hear or read that "Today's sunrise is at 6:50 a.m. and sunset at 4:58 p.m.," and when you look outside, you find that there is still light outside. By sunset it is meant the disappearance of the sun from the western horizon.

In the books of Bukhari and Muslim, the Messenger of Allah (saas) said: "The people will always remain in a good state of mind and body (during fast) so far as they hurry in the breaking of the fast and delaying the sahuur."

It is recommended also to break the fast with fresh dates, *rutub*, and in odd numbers, or *tamr*, regular table or supermarket dates, or water. If dates are not available, any fruit will do. If there is no food or drink to break the fast with, intend in your heart to break fast, and whenever food is available you should eat.

In a report by Anas (raa), he said: "The Prophet (saas) used to break fast with fresh, ripe dates *rutub*, before he offered his Maghrib prayer. If they were not available, he would break with regular dates, or drink water if there were no dates." (Abu Dawud Tirmidhi).

In this report, there is an indication that with the Messenger of Allah (saas) breaking fast precedes evening prayer, *Maghrib*, as if to say the last meal before fast precedes the morning prayer. Likewise, the first meal at the time of *iftaar*, the fast-breaking meal, precedes evening prayer, *Maghrib*. Hence, the procedure at *Iftar* goes like this: break with a light meal, preferably dates, make *Iqamah* for Maghrib prayer, then take your regular meal.

The meal, may be taken with the family at home, or friends and relatives may be invited to the *Iftar*, as we shall see charitable works are highly recommended in the month of Ramadan. Over the years phenomena have evolved in different masajid, and Islamic Centers in the United States of America and elsewhere, where arrangements are made by the believers to break fast in *jama'ah* in the masajid. These gatherings are excellent and are encouraged as they lead to Taraweeh prayer in *Jamaaah* in the masjid.

SUPPLICATIONS DURING AND AT BREAK TIME

The Lawgiver has recommended that the fasting person take the opportunity on this occasion and beseech Allah during the period of fasting, especially around the hour of breaking fast, *iftar*. He should request diligently, whatever he or she desires, from the Owner of creation, *Rabbil Alameen*.

In the book of Ibn Maja, Abdullah bin 'Amru bin 'Al-As (raa) reported that the Messenger of Allah (saas) said: "Indeed, as to the faster, about the time he breaks his fast, his *du'a*, (supplication) will not be turned away by Allah." This hadith reveals a special privilege afforded only to the servant who observes fasting and at the hour he brings his fasting to a close. Each fasting person has the right to supplication and the right that it will be answered, a promise from the One who never reneges on His promises.

However, granting the faster's *du'a* request falls within the conditions of *du'a*. That is, whatever you ask Allah (SWT), He will grant it in His own time, and when he knows that granting your request will not lead to your ruin. Do not ask of Him something unlawful.

In a report by Tirmidhi (raa), the Messenger of Allah (saas) has been reported as saying: "There are three categories of people whose *du'a* (supplications) will not be rejected: the person who observes the fast until he breaks, a just ruler, and the person who has been wronged." This citation supports the previous one, while adding that when prayers are offered during fasting, supplications are highly encouraged.

In addition to the faster, a ruler's acts of justice weigh heavily on the scale of good deeds *(mizaan)*. This is the person whose pronouncements, orders and decrees affect the lives of others. The ruler may be a political leader, a judge, or a community leader who does not abuse the power and authority invested in him. If any one of them makes a request, Allah (SWT) will swiftly grant it.

Conversely, on the reverse side, if the faster did not observe fasting properly, or the ruler abuses the power invested in him, their supplications will not only be turned away unanswered, but will incur the wrath of Allah.

The third person in the Hadith is *al-mazluum*. This is an individual who has been wronged, such as a victim of a crime against himself or his property, or if his civil rights have been violated, or he is a victim of fraud or any type of crime. If such a person raises his hands and asks Allah (SWT) for help, his or her prayer will be granted.

EXAMPLES OF SUPPLICATION DURING RAMADAN

It has been reported that the Messenger of Allah (saas) used to say the following:

اللّٰهُمَّ إِنِي أَسْأَلُكَ بِرَحْمَتِكَ آلَّتِى وَسِعَتْ كُلَ شَيْءٍ اَنْ تَغْـفِرَ لِى

Allahumma Inne as aluka birahma-tikal Latee wasi'at kulla shayin an Taghfirale''

O Allah, I request You by Your mercy that encompasses everything in the creation to forgive me.

Also:

ذَهَبَ الظَّمْأُ وَابْتَلَتِ الْعُرُوقُ وَ ثَبَتَ الْأَجْرُ اِنْ شَاءَ اللهُ تَـــعَالَى

''Dhahabaz Zamau, wabta latil'uruq, wa Thabatal Ajru In Sha Allah ta'ala.''

The thirst is gone and the throats are wet again and the reward is established, Allah willing.

Also:

اللّٰهُمَّ لَكَ صَمْتُ وَ بِكَ آمَنْتُ وَ عَلَيْكَ تَوَكَّلْتُ وَعَلَى رِزْقُكَ أَفْطَرْتُ

''Allahumma laka sumtu wabika a mantu wa'alaika Tawakaltu, wa'ala rizquka'' aftartu.

O Allah, I fasted for Your sake. I believed in You and relied on You and I break my fast on your provisions.

The above supplications have been reported from the Messenger of Allah (saas). Anyone of them may be said before you put the date or water in your mouth. Speaking of *iftar*, it is recommended to be in a state of purity, *(wudu)* before *iftar*, so that when the *adhan* is called for *Maghrib* prayer, anyone who hears the *adhan* should break fast immediately at the sound of *Allahu Akbar* and should not wait until the *adhan* is completed. The caller will break after *adhan*.

AVOIDANCE OF THE THINGS THAT CONTRADICT THE SPIRIT OF FASTING

Fasting is one of the best acts of worship. It is mandated by Allah (SWT) to purify the soul along with the practice of good deeds. Thus the faster ought to be aware of acts or behaviors that may spoil his fast so that he or she will attain the highest benefit physically and spiritually.

Fasting is not only restraining oneself from fast-breakers—food, drink and sex—these restrain only the mouth and the private parts. Every limb *(jawarih)* must be restrained. The tongue must desist from slander and back-biting. The eyes must restrain themselves from any unlawful look. The hand must not touch or take what does not belong to it. The ears must not listen to idle talk, gossip, lyrics and notes that contain obscene and indecent things; the nose must fast also by not sniffing, smelling unlawful things. The feet must fast by not going to places where sinful acts are propagated. When you eat *sahuur* and *iftar*, make sure the food on the table has been obtained lawfully. If the servant has observed the fast in these terms and acted accordingly, he or she will have gained positively by Ramadan and will receive the maximum reward.

Hence, fasting is a state of mind that transcends the physical restraint. In a hadith by Abu Hurairah, the Messenger of Allah (saas) said: "It is not fasting, just to restrain from food and drink, instead the fast is to cease from idle talk *(laghw)*, obscenity, and should anyone insult or provoke you, or act ignorantly towards you, respond to it by saying, 'I am fasting, I am indeed fasting.'" (Ibn Khuzaima)

In another citation reported by Abu Hurairah (raa) the Messenger of Allah, (saas), said: "He who does not stop from false talk or stop from acting upon false talk, Allah will have no need that he abstain from his food and drink." (Bukhari)

Again, in the same spirit, the Messenger of Allah (saas) said: "Many an observer of fasting will not receive from his fasting any reward but the pain of hunger, and many a night worshipper will not receive any reward from his prayer but the loss of sleep." (Nasaie and Hakim)

These three *(ahadith)* are evidence that the most important thing in the eyes of the Lawgiver is not merely physically restraining from the obvious food and drink, but the total commitment of the servant's body and soul to the letter and spirit of fasting. The curfew of the body and mind during the state of fasting enables the person who has fasted in the true spirit of Ramadan to have the necessary requirements to withstand the turbulence of life for the next eleven months.

When the Messenger of Allah (saas) said in the hadith, "Allah will have no need..." (Bukhari), he was indicating the depth or seriousness of this case. If you fail the test, Allah will have no need that you abstain...in that test. If Allah rejects the test, who else will accept it? Nobody! Hence, the pain of hunger and the burning of thirst will go unrewarded.

ORAL HYGIENE

It is recommended to take care of the mouth, teeth and gums all the time, and more so during fasting. This can be achieved by the use of *siwaak*, a special stick or root (from *Arak* tree) that is used to cleanse the teeth and strengthen the gums. Although the best *siwaak* is the one called *al-Arak* produced in Hijaz, in Arabia, it will suffice to use anything that will cleanse the teeth and remove the stain and refresh the mouth, like *halaal toothpaste*. In hadith by Abu Hurairah, the Prophet (saas) said: "Were not it because of fear of burdening my community (Ummah) I would have commanded them to use *siwaak* (brush their teeth with a chewing stick) before every ablution." (Malik)

In another hadith by 'Aishah (raa) the Messenger of Allah (saas) said: "*Siwak* cleanses the mouth and pleases Allah." (Ahmad). Yet, in another report by Amir bin Rabeelah (raa), he said: "I saw the Messenger of Allah (saas) on numerous occasions chewing *siwaak* while fasting." (Tirmidhi)

In the first and second hadith, the importance of oral hygiene is underscored and encouraged on every occasion: before *wudu* for regular prayer, before reciting *Al-Qur'an*, before or after sleeping, when the mouth odor changes and, of course, during fasting. The third hadith indicates the Prophet (saas) took care of his teeth during the time of fasting.

THE USE OF TOOTHPASTE

Many scholars consider the use of toothpaste during the period of fasting as undesirable *(makruuh)*, because it is a thorough or rather extensive way of cleaning the teeth. This would have been all right if not because of the fasting. The reason why thorough cleaning is considered makruuh is because of the fear of swallowing water as one attempts to rinse and flush out the taste and soapy residue of toothpaste. This fear is justified by hadith reported by Laqit bin Sabrah (raa) that the Messenger of Allah said: "Perfect your Wudu, clean between your fingers and sniff water thoroughly unless you are fasting." (Abu Dawud and Nasa'e)

CATEGORIES OF FASTERS

The faster excels in the degree and the depth of his fasting in proportion to the intent and in the way he communicates with Allah as well adheres to the rules of fasting. Ibn Rajab (raa) stated the people who observe the fasting are of two categories.

One who abstains from food and drink and sexual desires for the sake of Allah. in so doing, he desires a return from Allah in a form of paradise, *Jannah*. He resembles a businessman who trades, bargains and deals with Allah (swt). Allah in turn will not neglect nor deny him his due reward. For no one whoever deals or trades with Allah ever lost a thing. Instead, the person will be rewarded a great deal more. The Messenger (saas) told a man: "When you abstain from anything for the fear of Allah, He will substitute for you something better." (Ahmed)

The faster will receive in paradise what he wishes of food, drinks and desires. Allah (swt) states: "Eat ye and drink ye with full satisfaction because of a (good) that ye sent before you in the days that are gone." (Al-Qur'an, 69:24) According to Imam Mujahid this verse referees to the righteous faster. In a hadith the Messenger saw Abdur Rahmam bin Samrah in a vision, he said: "I saw a man from my community lolling his tongue for thirst, whenever he comes near to water fountain he is denied a drink and sacked, then fasting of Ramadan came and gave him water and quenched him." (Tabranee)

The other category is the believer who fasts by abstaining from worldly things for Allah. His heart fasts from grief and greed for material possessions, his mind fasts from wishful thinking while his heart and soul are ever fresh with the remembrance of Allah and the Final Day. This faster's *iftar*, fast-break, is when he or she meets Allah, and his happiness is when he sees his Maker. This is fasting of *khawasul khawas*, specials of the specials, the *aarifeen*, truly wise and knowing.

The *aarifeen*, truly wise, are the people who are not entertained nor gratified by material earthly things, no sound, sight, or shape can gratify them beside Allah. No ocean can quench their thirst but the continence of Allah, their ambitions are bigger than this world. In a nut shell whoever fasts by the command of Allah from lusts for food, drink, and desires, Allah will greet him in the Hereafter, in the *Jannah*, and whoever fasts from anything but Allah his final Eid will be when he is granted the ultimate honor of seeing his Lord. Allah states:

"For those whose hopes are in the meeting with Allah (in the Hereafter, let them strive) for the term (appointed) by Allah is surely coming and He hears and knows all things."
(Al-Qur'an, 29:5)

CHARITY *(SADAQAH)*

The acts of charity and benevolence toward the less fortunate, for the sake of Allah, are highly desired on all occasions, but more so during the blessed month of Ramadan. In the book of *Al-Bukhari*, Ibn 'Abbas (raa) related: "The Messenger of Allah (saas) is the most benevolent among the people. His benevolence increases markedly during the month of Ramadan when the angel Jibreel meets him every night of Ramadan, to rehearse with him the *Holy Qur'an*. The Messenger of Allah (saas) was more charitable with his good possessions than the moving winds that bring torrential rain."

As you may be aware, there are two kinds of charitable acts. There is regular, voluntary charity, *(sadaqah)*, that can be given any time, from inviting others to meals at *iftar* time during Ramadan, to outright gifts to an individual or a charitable organization. On the other hand, there is an obligation of *Zakaat* (obligatory charity), which is the annual return of 2.5 percent that is levied against one's savings or assets that have matured in the last twelve months. Although annual calendars for Zakat can be set in any month, many people prefer to give their *Zakaat* to its rightful owners during Ramadan so as to offer these two obligations of Islam at the same time. We included a brief Fiqh of Zakaat and its recipients in the book.

RECITATION OF AL-QUR'AN (TILAWATUL QUR'AN)

It is highly recommended to recite or read the entire *Al-Qur'an*, the final word of Allah (SWT), at all times, at least completing it twice in a year. The reports from the companions show how some of them completed *Al-Qur'an* in five days, some in four while others in three days. Imam An-Nawawi (raa) said: "The speed by which one completes *Al-Qur'an* must depend on the condition and situation of the person and what he or she does for a living." The recitation of *Al-Qur'an* should not be the reason to become slacked in your other responsibilities. The speed of your recitation must be regulated by the ability to understand, because *Al-Qur'an* encourages the reciter to ponder about what he or she reads. Allah states: "Here is a Book which We have sent down unto thee, full of blessings, that they may meditate on its signs, and that men of understanding may receive admonition." (*Al-Qur'an, 38:29*)

This verse indicates that *Al-Qur'an* was revealed for the maximum encyclopedic benefit, mercy, and guidance to the human race. That is why He (SWT) described it as blessed, (*mubarak*). These blessings can be realized to the fullest only if the reader meditates and thinks through its divine words, containing layers of insights and wisdom and life-long experiences of the human race — of how to live a better life both spiritually and materially — which can never be found in any other book.

In a hadith by 'Aishah (raa), reported by Al-Baihaqi, she said: "The house in which *Al-Qur'an* is recited is seen by the heavenly world as the stars are seen by the earthly world." This hadith indicates some of the meritorious aspects of this most authenticated book of Allah. The home in which its residents recite this book is illuminated as brightly as a star on the face of the earth, and is visible in outer space.

As a preparation for reading, it is recommended to have cleanliness, (*taharah*), by making *wudu* before settling down to recite *Al-Qur'an*. for the recitation of *Al-Qur'an* is worship, *'ebadah*, namely the best form of remembrance of Allah (*dhikir*). The Messenger of Allah (saas) disliked making *dhikir* without cleanliness. Allah (SWT) states in *Al-Qur'an*: "And that is indeed a mighty adjuration, if you but knew. That this is indeed a *Qur'an* most honorable, in a book well-guarded, which none shall touch but those who are clean." (*Al-Quran 56:76–79*).

It is not a sin, however, to read without *wudu* if you are unclean from minor impurities that entail *wudu* before prayer. If you feel like using the restroom for urination, passing wind, etc., stop and go relieve yourself completely, and make Wudu then return to resume your reading. If you are defiled from major impurities, that is, the ones which entail complete bath, *(ghusl)*, it is prohibited to read *Al-Qur'an* during the state of defilement, the agents of which include discharge of semen, sexual intercourse, bleeding as a result of childbirth, and menstruation. However, it is allowed for these people to look in *Al-Qur'an* while not holding it, and they may read it with their eyes and their hearts, but not recite it. Note: one shouldn't encourage reading *Qur'an* in a state of defilement, until *Ghusl* is performed first.

The place you choose to sit to recite *Al-Qur'an* should be clean from any filth or bad odor. This is why it is prohibited to read it the restroom. While reading the *Qur'an*, it is recommended to face the direction of *Al-Qiblah*.

The reciters are commanded to say, I seek refuge, *"Ta'awwudh,"* that is, putting a distance between themselves and Satan *(Shaytan)* by seeking refuge in Allah (SWT) from the rejected enemy, the reason being Satan dislikes to see a servant in communication with Allah. If you do not seek refuge, he may come to distract, confuse, and induce you to doubt. Allah (SWT) says: "When you do read *Al-Qur'an*, seek Allah's protection from Satan, the rejected." *(Al-Qur'an 16:98)* In the event that you are interrupted during reading, it is advisable to repeat *ta'awwudh* before you resume. As for the phrase of *ta'awwudh*, the following is reported:

$$\text{أَعُوذُ بِاللهِ السَّمِيعِ الْعَلِيمِ مِنَ الشَّيْطَانِ الرَّجِيمِ}$$

Auwudhu billahi　　　　　　　I seek refuge with Allah The All
(As-Samee'u Al-'Aleem)　　　Hearing, The All-Knowing, from
minash Shaitan ir Rajeem.　　Satan, the rejected.

The majority of scholars recommend that it be said aloud, especially if there is an audience.

In Islam we are commanded to start every act, spiritual or non-spiritual, big or small, with *Basmalah*, that is: *"Bis mil llahir-Rahmanir-Raheem"* (In the Name of Allah, Most Gracious, Most

Merciful.) The reason is to seek Allah's blessings for the action you are about to embark on. Undoubtedly, no deed is more deserving or worthy of *Basmalah* than the *'ebadah* of reading *Al-Qur'an*. With the revelation of *Bismillahir-Rahmanir Raheem*, Allah has educated His Messenger (saas) to make it an unceasing habit of saying *Bismallah* before reading and before every act.

Basmalah is one of the unique aspects of *Al-Qur'an* as every chapter *(surah)*, except Surah Nine *(Tawbah)* commences with this most profound statement. It is prearranged as an incomplete statement to be completed, or filled in, if you will, by the servant. For instance, if you want to read, it becomes: I read in the Name of Allah...if you want to eat, it becomes: I eat in the Name of Allah...That is what we mean by an incomplete statement to be completed by the doer.

If you can read *Al-Qur'an* in the Arabic language, it is preferred to recite with the basic rules of *tajweed*, including rules of chanting *(al-ghunnah)*, prolongations *(al-madd)*, assimilation *(al-idghaam)*, etc. In a report by Bukhari, Anas bin Malik (raa) was asked to describe the way of the Messenger of Allah (saas) in reciting *Al-Qur'an*. Anas said the Messenger of Allah (saas) used to recite with *tarteel*, chanting, prolonging his long vowels. Anas (raa) gave a demonstration by reciting *'Bismallah'* to show how the Messenger (saas) recited it, prolonging the sublime word, Allah, Ar-Rahman, and Ar-Raheem.'"

It is, however, undesirable to read with excessive speed. Reading a part of *Al-Qur'an*, *(juzh)*, slowly, so as to think through what you read, is preferred to reading double the ordinary speed without pondering. The former way is more respectful, and is in accord with the aims of the Lawgiver, than hastily reading through the Book absent-mindedly.

It is recommended to beautify your recital with a pleasant voice. In a hadith by Ibn Hibban (raa), the Messenger of Allah (saas) has been reported as saying: "Beautify the recitation of your *Qur'an* with your voices." But you should not exaggerate to the point that the phonics, morphology, or syntax are distorted or altered. Reciting *Al-Qur'an* with mistakes, *(lahn)* is not synonymous with chanting or a pleasing voice. Also, one's recitation should not sound like singing.

I mentioned earlier that it is sunnah to seek to comprehend what you read. The following are some of the ways one should go about *tadabur*, or pondering through what he reads. The simplest thing is to think out the meaning of the words so as to get a better insight to their meaning and message.

If the verse contains commands and prohibitions you should immediately decide to accept or restrain from them. But if it is something you have failed in the past to do, you should seek forgiveness and intend to do it in the future. In the event that the verse contains mercy, you should feel happy and request it, or if it contains wrath, you should seek refuge in Allah. If the verse glorifies Allah, you should glorify Him.

In the book of Muslim, Huzaifah bin Yaman is reported as saying: "I prayed behind the Messenger of Allah (saas) one night. He opened his recitation after *Al-Fatihah* with chapter *Al-Baqarah*, the Cow. Coming to the end of it, he followed it with the chapter *An-Nisa*, the Women. Coming to its end, he followed it with Chapter *Al-'Emran*, the Family of Emran). He read them consecutively and when he came to a verse that contained glorification of Allah, he glorified, or a question, he asked, or seeking refuge he sought refuge."

It is sunnah to say *takbeer* from *Chapter Ad-Duha, 93* to the end *An-Nas, Chapter 114*. The sunnah is to pause at the end of *Chapter 93* then say *Takbeer*. If you are completing *Al-Qur'an*, you do likewise at the end of each *surah*, chapter, until *An-Nas*. The sunnah was started after the first revelation was received and after the period of *Fatrah*, during which revelation was cut off from the Prophet (saas), and the Makkans were saying Allah had forsaken Muhammad. When *Ad-Duha* was revealed, the Messenger of Allah (saas) said: *"Allahu Akbar"* (Allah is the Greatest).

As to what one should say: You may say *"Allahu Akbar"* (Allah is the Greatest), or *La Illaha illallah, wallahu Akbar*, (There is no deity but Allah, and Allah is the Greatest).

The sunnah recommends prostrating at the end of every *sajdah* (prostration verse). There are 15 such verses in *Al-Qur'an*. They are in chapters: *Al-Aaraaf*, (7:206); *Ar-Ra'ad*, (13:15); *An-Nahl*, (16:49); *Al-Isra*, (17:107); *Maryam*, (19:58); *Al-Hajj*, (22:18 and 22:77); *Al-Furqan*, (25:60); *An-Naml*, (27:77); *As-Sajdah*, (32:15); *Saad*, (38:24); *Fussilat*, (41:37); *An-Najm*, (53:62); *Al-Insiqaq*, (84:21); and *Al-'Alaq*, (96:19).

Now there is the question about what is the best time to read or recite *Al-Qur'an*. The best time by far is reciting during *Salaat*, then night-time reading, especially the latter part of it. The best time of day is after *Subh* (Morning Prayer). The best or preferred days are the days of 'Arafah, Fridays, Mondays, and Thursdays. The best ten days are the last ten of Ramadan and first ten days of the month, Zul-Hijjah. Of the months, Ramadan is the best.

The preferred day to start Al-Qur'an is Friday, and the best day to complete it is Thursday. The best hour to complete it is the first part of the day or night. For, according to Sa'ad bin Abi Waqqaas (raa), if the completion is in the first part of the night, the angels will pray for you until morning, and if it is early in the morning they will pray for you until evening. Fasting is recommended on the day of completion.

It is recommended to start again after each completion of Al-Qur'an. In a hadith reported by Tirmidhi (raa), the Messenger of Allah (saas) has been reported as saying: "The best deeds in the sight of Allah are the deeds of the one who completes Qur'an and resumes again, the one who reads Al-Qur'an from the beginning to the end, and whenever he finishes he resumes again."

It is undesirable to stop reading to converse or talk to someone, laugh or play or look at something that takes away your attention, unless there is a valid reason, as has been reported by Al-Bukhari, by the way of Ibn 'Umar (raa).

DU'AA OF RECITATION OF THE ENTIRE QUR'AN (DU'AA KHATMIL QURAN)

At the completion of Al-Qur'an starting from Al-Fatihah to An-Nas the reciter must turn to Almighty Allah with supplications. It is further advisable to gather the members of ones entire family and friends for these special supplications. This may be done in a house or in the masjid. In a hadith reported by Anas bin Malik (raa) the Messenger of allah (saas) said: "The supplication of the completion of qur'anic recitation is an accepted supplication." (Abu-Dawud) Hence forth, Anas was accustomed to gather his family to pray. He will supplicate while they say ameen. Indeed, du'aa is not a set of recitations that one is suppose to read on different occasions, it is a dynamic interaction between the supplicant and His Creator. When you list your requests and needs take them to the Hearkener (Al-Mujeeb).

There is no special supplication reported from the Messenger of Allah (saas) at the completion of the entire Qur'an recitation. The believer is free to supplicate, pray or request in supplication whatever one desires of this world or the Hereafter. The supplications that are in circulation and are found at the end of certain publications are not reported or related to the Messenger of Allah, nor from his companions, or the followers of the companions or even from the four famous Imams of Islamic thought, Abu Hanifah, Malik, Shafi'e and Ahmed bin Hambal may Allah's mercy be upon them.

The supplicant must be aware of what he is saying in the supplication. He must believe in the supplication being answered by Allah, supplicate with sincerity and determination, and must not doubt in the supplication.

It is recommended that the suppliant dresses well in clean garment, sit well, and face the *qiblah*, and choose of supplications in Al-Qur'an like the saying of the Almighty Allah in chapter Al-Baqarah: "...Our Lord give us good in this world and good in the hereafter and defend us from the torment of the fire." (Al-Qur'an, 2: 201) Or what has been reported from the Messenger because he was given the best composition of words and phrases.

STRIVING IN DEVOTION IN THE LAST TEN DAYS OF RAMADAN

Allah, the Almighty, in His mercy and wisdom, favored certain hours, days, and months with His benevolence. Among these months, Ramadan is the month of favor, the month of *Al-Qur'an*. Of the days of Ramadan, the last ten days are the most meritorious for the acts of recitation of *Al-Qur'an*, nightly Sunnah prayers, etc., which weigh heavily on the scale of deeds, *(mizaan)*. After all, as we will see, in this month and during these last ten days, and in one of the odd numbered days, the annual return of deeds takes place, this night is known as the Night of Power (Laylatul Qadir).

In a hadith by Bukhari and Muslim, the Messenger's wife related that: "When the month of Ramadan enters its last ten days, the Messenger of Allah (saas) spends his night praying and wakes up his family to join him, and he would tighten his belt."

In this hadith, we see how the Messenger's wife, 'Aishah, (raa), informed us of what took place in her house during the last ten days of Ramadan. This was not the right time for the eyes to get their fill in sleep. The Prophet (saas) didn't do this alone. His whole family was involved and the hadith used the word "tighten his belt" in its figurative sense to mean an all-out seriousness of the devotion.

THINGS PERMITTED DURING FAST

Although fasting entails restriction and abstinence there are certain things that are permitted for the faster to do. They include:

Bathing *(Al-Ghusul)*, provided extra caution is taken to prevent water being swallowed by the mouth or nose.

'Aishah (raa) reported that: "The Messenger of Allah (saas) used to wake up defiled with semen while fasting, then he took his bath." (Bukhari and Muslim)

In another hadith, the Messenger of Allah (saas) has been seen pouring water on his head while he was fasting to minimize the thirst and heat.

These two reports prove that bathing are lawful during the fast, regardless of the reason, whether to cool the body or for cleanliness. Ibn Umar (raa) has been reported to have wet a cloth and covered his body with it. Anas bin Malik (raa) used to have a pool and he used to jump into it to cool his body.

Coloring the eyelids, **Al-Khul**, or using eye drops, such as Visine, is permitted whether the solution reaches the throat or not, the reason being the eyes are not the regular passage for food or nourishment. The strength of this case lies on the report by Anas bin Malik, (raa), who was the Messenger's cook for life. Anas used to color his eyes with kuhl while fasting.

Being in the company of the Prophet (saas) for that long, while coloring the eyes, the Prophet would have seen him and corrected him if it was wrong. So is the case with ear drops or any medicine being applied on open wounds, whether the person feels it in the throat or not, because these things are not food or drink, nor are they substitutes. The above is the understanding of many scholars, including Imams Shafi'e, Abu Hanifah and Sheikh Ibn 'Taymiyah (raa).

Kissing *(Qublah)*. For married couples, expressing affection toward each other by kissing is inevitable. It may take place any time, day or night. To deny or prohibit this feeling during Ramadan would undoubtedly lead to some hardship. Therefore, the Lawgiver permitted a man to kiss his spouse on the cheek, hand, or mouth or hold hand and embrace, if he feels like it and can control his feelings. The Messenger's wife Aishah (raa) reported: "The Messenger (saas) used to kiss while fasting and to embrace while fasting, but he was the most able person to control his desire." (Tirmidhi, Bukhari, Muslim)

In another report by 'Umar (raa), he stated: "I felt the urge one day during fast, so I kissed (my wife). After realizing what I had done, I went to the Messenger of Allah (saas) and informed him that I had committed a great sin by kissing while fasting. The Messenger responded: Do you break fast if you rinse your mouth with water?' Umar said, No, nothing is wrong with rinsing.' Then, the Messenger said, Why bother?'" (Ahmed/Abu-Dawuud)

Inferring from this hadith, many scholars among the companions see nothing wrong with kissing, provided the believer can control his feelings. If he cannot control himself, kissing becomes *haraam* (unlawful) because it leads to unlawful acts. This general rule is known in Islamic jurisprudence as *saduz zaree'ah* (closing the door that may lead to unlawful acts). The fear of getting carried away leads some scholars to say kissing is undesirable *(makruuh)* and one better not do it for fear of ejaculation.

Rinsing Mouth *(Madmadah)* Is one of the procedures of ablution (wudu). Therefore, the faster is permitted to rinse his mouth and cleanse his nose by sniffing in water and blowing it out. However, during fasting the process should be applied lightly for fear of swallowing water. The Messenger of Allah (saas) said: "...If you sniff water through your nose do it thoroughly unless you are fasting." (Abu Dawuud)

This hadith indicates two things: the faster who is making *wudu* or just wants to rinse his mouth should do it with utmost caution lest he may swallow the water and invalidate his fast. The hadith is a proof that the nose is a regular passage, like the mouth, of nourishment and as such takes it rules. Thus, if water passes through the mouth or nose to the stomach, the fast is invalidated. Not so with the eyes or ears.

But what if, during rinsing, you swallow water? Does that break the fast? If water reaches the throat unintentionally, or without negligence on your parts, the fast is still valid, but if water is swallowed intentionally, the fast is nullified.

THINGS PERMITTED TO THE FASTER AS UNAVOIDABLE

Things that are a part of daily living, such as swallowing saliva, mucus, street dust, or mill dust (for workers at the mill), are unavoidable, and they do not nullify the fast. Also, tasting of foods by cooks or tasting it with intention to buy, provided the food is not swallowed, but spat out. Nor is the fast affected by smelling a perfume or using it on the body or cloth. But intentionally sniffing any particles that might travel through the nose to the belly would spoil the fast.

The faster is allowed to eat and drink and have sexual intercourse from sundown until the break of dawn. When dawn breaks and there is food in the mouth, it should be spat out and one should cease from ejaculation. If one swallows the food or continues to have sex, his fast is nullified. In a hadith by Muslim and Bukhari (raa) reported by 'Aisha (raa) the Messenger of Allah (saas) said: "When Bilal calls adhan at night eat and drink until Ibn Ulmm Maktum calls."

The hadith indicates that there used to be two adhans; the first one was announced by Bilal Ibn Rabah (raa). The purpose of which was two fold: to wake the believers up for *sahuur* and to indicate the period of *sahuur*; and Abdullah Ibn Umm-Maktum's to announce the time to stop eating and prepare for morning prayer.

For women, bleeding as a result of menstruation, or postchild birth, if the blood stops, they may delay their bathing (ghusl) until daybreak and they may wake up fasting, but they should cleanse themselves, before performing prayer, Salaat.

NULLIFIERS OF THE FAST

There are two categories of nullifiers of fast:

1. nullifiers that entail redemption (*qadaa*).
2. nullifiers that entail redemption of the day or days invalidated (*qadaa*), and expiation, (*kaffarah*).

NULLIFIERS THAT ENTAIL REDEMPTION (AL-QADAA)

The first nullifiers are when the fast is rendered invalid and it must be redeemed after Ramadan in a period extending over eleven months, but no later than the next Ramadan.

The nullifiers are:

1. **Intentionally eating** or **drinking** by allowing food and drink to travel through the mouth or nose to the stomach. When this happens, the fast is nullified, even if it is just a bite or a sip.

On the other hand, if eating or drinking occurs unintentionally, by mistake, and, for example, if a person forgetfully drinks
after jogging, the fast is correct and resumes and no redemption
is necessary provided the faster does not continue to eat or drink
after he remembers. This ruling rests on the hadith narrated by
many reporters by way of Abu Hurairah (raa) that the Prophet
(saas) said: "Whoever forgets—while fasting—and eats or
drinks, should stop immediately and resume or complete his
fast. For he has just been fed and quenched by Allah." (Agreed
Upon)

The hadith indicates there is no need to worry if forgetfulness
overcomes a faster causing him or her to eat or drink. Besides,
Allah (SWT), in His mercy, justifies the person continuing to fast
because the sustenance that he took was a direct gift from Allah,
to the faster. The believers must be aware that this phenomenon
occurs usually in the first few days of the fast, before the body
and the mind adjust themselves to the new eating schedule.

2. **A substitute for food and drink** is as good a nullifier of fast
as the real thing. By food substitute we mean two things:

Giving a faster a blood transfusion due to the loss of blood
resulting from an injury, invalidates the fast, the reason being
blood is a form of nourishment like food. Is not one of the reasons
for eating to get blood flowing within our system?

Feeding an individual through the stomach, or intravenously,
(through the veins), parenteral feeding (injecting nutrients into
the body) as a substitute for food and drink invalidates the fast.
Because this is substitute for food, it takes its case in nullifying
the fast.

3. **Inducing vomiting nullifies the fast.** By this is meant,
intentionally causing the contents of the stomach to be ejected
through the mouth either by wringing the stomach, or palpating
the throat, or by smelling or looking at an emetic substance. In
this case, the fast should be redeemed later or after Ramadan, but
if the fast is a Sunnah fast, one has a choice to make it up later or
not. In a hadith related by Abu Hurairah (raa) the Messenger of
Allah (saas) said: "Whoever is overcome by vomiting wouldn't
have to make it up, but if vomiting is the result of inducement
(the fast is invalidated) and would have to be made up." (Ahmed)

It is important to say that the amount of the ejected contents,
whether it is little or much, has no effect on the ruling.

One of the reasons why induced vomiting invalidates fasting is when the contents of the belly are thrown up, the body, which is already short on nourishment, is further weakened. Therefore, the Lawgiver as a mercy tells the believer to go ahead and break this day, and make it up later.

However, no faster should break his fast because he or she feels nausea, until the vomiting actually occurs.

4. **Bleeding as a result of menstruation** (known as *hayd*), or post childbirth bleeding, *(nifaas)*, nullifies the fast, even if it occurs moments before sunset, and before iftar time. In this case, the fast is no longer valid, and even if the woman tried to continue, it would still not be valid. It has been reported that the Prophet (saas) said regarding menstruation, "When a woman experiences her monthly period, she will not pray or fast, but she shall redeem the fast after Ramadan, but not Salaat."

5. **Ejaculation of semen, as a result of kissing**, hugging, using the hand (as in self-pollution) or using any object for a sexual purpose for both men and women invalidates the fast because this is *shahawah*, a sensuous or lustful act that nullifies the fast. In a hadith *Al-Qudsi*, the Messenger of Allah (saas) has been reported as saying referring to the faster: "He who abstains from his food, his drink and his lustful desires for My (Allah) sake." *(Al-Bukhari)*

But if ejaculation occurs as result of a wet dream, or just unintentional thinking that is devoid of actual acts or inducements, the fast remains valid. Allah (SWT) will not hold one responsible for things randomly thought of which do not accompany the deed. The Messenger of Allah (saas) said: "Verily, Allah has pardoned my community, (Ummah) what their souls entertain in so far as they do not do or speak." (Agreed upon) This citation is referring to the case of thoughts borne in mind. There are bad thoughts and good thoughts. The bad thoughts and intentions are left unpunished so far as they are not rendered into deeds, a blessing from Him (SWT). For were He to hold us accountable for our thoughts, man would not have been able to escape His wrath. On the other hand, a good thought is rewarded regardless of whether the thought is being rendered into deed or not.

In a hadith, related by Ibn Abbas (raa) the Messenger of Allah (saas) conveying the Message from His Lord, says: "Allah has written down the good deeds and the bad ones. Then He explained it (by saying that) he who has intended a good deed and not done it, Allah records it with Himself as a full good deed, but if he has intended it and has done it, Allah records it with Himself as from ten good deeds, multiplied to seven hundred times, or many times over. But if he has intended a bad deed and has not done it, Allah records it with Himself as a full good deed, but if he has intended it, and has done it, Allah records it as one bad deed." (Bukhari/Muslim)

NULLIFIERS THAT ENTAIL REDEMPTION AND EXPIATION (AL-QADA & KAFFARAH)

When a faster intentionally has marital relations with his wife during the daytime, the fast is invalidated. This is the most serious of fast-breakers. That is why, besides redeeming the day, there is *kaffarah mughallazah*, severe expiation to be observed after Ramadan.

There is a precedent to this case during the time of the Prophet (saas) as related by Abu Hurairah (raa) who said a man came to the Messenger of Allah, and said: "'I am ruined, O Messenger of Allah.' The Prophet (saas) asked Him, 'What ruins you?' He replied: 'I had marital relations with my wife in Ramadan.' The Messenger of Allah (saas) asked him, 'Do you have a bondsman to free as an expiation?' He said 'No.' The Messenger of Allah (saas) asked him again, 'Are you able to fast two consecutive months?' 'No,' he said. The Messenger of Allah (saas) asked again, 'Do you have enough to feed sixty poor people?' 'No,' he said. As the Messenger of Allah (saas) sat, someone brought a sack full of dates. The Messenger of Allah (saas) gave the dates to the man and told him to expiate with it (by giving it to the poor). The man said, 'Is there anyone poorer than I am, within the innermost part of this city? Indeed, there is no household in more desperate need than us.' The Messenger of Allah (saas) laughed until his teeth and gums could be seen. He said to him, 'Then go and feed your family.'" (Jama'ah, including Bukhari and Muslim)

This hadith indicates many important points. First, what constitutes expiation is one of the three following things:

1. Freeing a person in bondage, man or woman. If a man did not have a bondaman, he could purchase one and set him free. By the way, this was one way Islam combatted the institution of slavery.

2. Fasting two consecutive months.

3. Feeding sixty poor people an average meal. Indeed, the severity of the penalty is indicative of how serious the offense is.

According to *Jamhur*, the majority of the scholars, both the man and his wife are responsible for making up the expiation, provided both intentionally committed the offense during the daytime, while both had intended to fast that day. But, if he forced his wife during Ramadan to have relations with him, both will redeem the day, but he will be the one to expiate. If she is not observing fast for some reason, there will be nothing due on her.

Others said, regardless of whether he forced her or not, only the man should expiate because in the hadith, the Messenger (saas) commanded the man, not the woman, to expiate. However, the previous explanation is stronger.

Another point discussed is which is the best among the three choices of expiation: freeing, fasting, or feeding? Whichever is easier to the expiator is the one he should do. There is another hadith by Abu Hurairah (raa) in which the Messenger of Allah (saas) told a man who broke his fast to free a person, or fast two consecutive months, or feed sixty indigent. This report, by the way of Muslim, demonstrated that one has a choice.

What happens to a person who had sex during fasting, but before he expiates he repeats the offense? How many expiations should he make? There will be only one expiation. It is like in prayer when a worshipper makes two mistakes in one prayer, he makes only one correction. But if he has expiated for the first offense and then repeated the offense, the scholars agreed that expiation is due for the second offense. The *Jamhur* of scholars infers from hadith that the expiation is dropped because of poverty. Allah is the best knower.

What happens to a person who has sex during fasting, but before he expiates he repeats the offense? How many expiations should he make? There will be only one expiation. It is like in prayer when a worshipper makes two mistakes in one prayer, he makes only one correction. But if he has expiated for the first offense and then repeated the offense, the scholars agreed that expiation is due for the second offense. The *Jamhur* of scholars infers from hadith that the expiation is dropped because of poverty. Allah is the best knower.

CONDITIONS OF FAST BREAKERS

The fast-breakers, except menstruation *(hayd)* and post child-birth bleeding *(nifaas)*, including marital relations, self-pollution, eating and drinking; indulging in them do not break fast and require redemption of the fast unless three conditions are met:

(1) Knowledge *(Elim)*

The person should have full knowledge that what he is about to do will invalidate his fast. If he is ignorant and does not know, the fast remains valid. Allah (SWT) said, "...But there is no blame on you if you make a mistake therein: (What counts) is the intentions of your hearts." *(Al-Qur'an, 33:5)*

Doubting the Break of Dawn

In the case of the ignorant person mentioned above, he can be either **(a)** ignorant of the Islamic rule in the matter, as a person who did not know that a certain act will invalidate fast, **or (b)** ignorant of the time, as a person who thinks the dawn has not broken and continues his *sahur*, finding out later that the sun has risen. Or he mistakenly breaks fast thinking the sun has set. In all these instances, the fast is valid, despite the ruling to the contrary by the majority of the scholars.

In a hadith by Bukhari (raa) when the following verse was revealed: "...And eat and drink, until the white thread of dawn appears to you distinct from its black thread..." (Al-Qur'an, 2:187)

Adyi bin Hatim (raa) told the Messenger of Allah (saas) that he placed two threads, one black and the other white, under this pillow as he sat to eat his sahuur. He continued to eat while glancing at the thread under his pillow to see whether he can differentiate between them. By the time he could differentiate between them, it was already daybreak. When he finished this story, the Messenger of Allah commented and explained: "Your pillow must be very vast (to cover the spaces of white and black threads). What is really meant is the whiteness of the day and the darkness of the night."

The point of reference in this hadith is that 'Adyi ate after *Fajr* and after the time he was supposed to stop, but the Prophet (saas) did not ask him to make up the day because he was ignorant of the Shari'ah rule. In another report by Bukhari Asma bint Abu Bakar (raa) said: "We broke fast one day in Ramadan, on a cloudy evening during the time of the Prophet, but after a while the sun appeared." Again in this citation there is no report that the Prophet commanded those who mistakenly broke their fast to make up the day. If he had, it would have been reported because of its importance.

Elsewhere, Hisham bin Urwah (raa), who was one of the reporters of the above hadith, said: "They were not commanded to redeem the day."

(2) Remembering (Dhikir)

The faster should remember before an act that it will invalidate his fast. If he forgets, the fast remains valid and resumes, as mentioned earlier.

Allah (SWT) states: "...Our Lord! condemn us not if we forget or fall into error..." (Al-Qur'an, 2:286) In Islam no one is condemned for an act done out of forgetfulness or due to a mistake. It is human, after all, to forget. In a hadith mentioned earlier it was observed: "Whoever forgets while fasting and eats or drinks, he should complete his fast (of that day), for he has just been fed and quenched by Allah." (Muslim and others)

Thus, regarding the eating and drinking of one who forgets, it is evident that he is not to be held responsible for his action. However, if he remembers or has been reminded, he should stop immediately, for if he continues to eat after that moment, the fast is invalid. Therefore, it is incumbent on anyone who sees a faster eating or drinking to remind him or her. Allah (SWT) said: "... Help you one another in righteousness and piety." (Al-Qur'an, 5:2)

(3) Breaking Fast Willingly (Ikhtiyaar)

For the fast to become invalid, the person should break on his own accord, eating or drinking intentionally without force from anyone. For, if he is coerced under the threat of harm, the fast remains valid. Allah (SWT) states: "Anyone who, after accepting faith in Allah, utters unbelief, except under coercion, his heart remaining firm in faith..." (Al-Qur'an, 16:106)

The point of reference here is if Allah absolves one from blame for claiming disbelief under compulsion (a person who has said a word of great sin), a person under similar conditions who has committed a lesser offense deserves pardon. Besides, the Messenger of Allah (saas) said in a hadith related by Ibn Abbas (raa): "Allah absolves my community (Ummah) from responsibility if they make a mistake, or forget, or have been forced to do something against their own will." (Ibn Majah) Relying on this citation, if, for instance, water is mistakenly swallowed during rinsing of the mouth or sniffing, or a person is forced under threat of harm to eat, the fast remains valid.

DUTIES AFTER RAMADAN

As the blessed month of Ramadan nears its end, there are three important obligations to help the faster bid the month a deserving farewell. These obligations also bring the faster closer to Allah, elevate his *Iman* and increase the weight of his deeds. These duties are: *Zakaatul-Fitr,* (Fast-breaking alms); *Takbeer,* (utterance of Allah is the Greatest), and Eid Prayer, (Festival of fast-breaking).

Fast Breaking Alms *(Zakaatul-Fitr)*

Allah (SWT) has mandated the observation of fast-breaking alms *(Zakaatul-Fitr)* at the end of Ramadan before Eid Prayer. Although this obligation was established by the Messenger (saas), it has the power of all the established commands of Allah, for the power to legislate and prescribe a rule has been granted to the Messenger of Allah, by Allah (SWT), Who states: "He who obeys the Messenger, obeys Allah; but if any turn away, We have not sent thee to watch over their (evil) deeds." (Quran, 4:80)

Also, "If anyone contends with the Messenger, even after guidance has been plainly conveyed to him, and follows a path other than that becoming to men of faith..." *(Al-Qur'an 4:115)* Also, "... So take what the Messenger assigns to you, and deny yourselves that which he withholds from you..." *(Al-Qur'an, 59:7)*

Eligibility

The giving of the fast-breaking alms is mandatory on every Muslim, old, young, man and woman, etc. In a hadith related by Abdullah bin 'Umar (raa) he said: "The Messenger of Allah, has commanded the faster to observe Ramadan fast-breaking alms, one *Sa'a,* (a beaker, a unit of measurement about two kilos and forty grams) of dates, barley on a bondsman, a freeman, on every man and woman, young and old..." (Bukhari/Muslim)

This citation indicates that the eligible people who should give these alms, are virtually every living Muslim, provided he or she possesses more than the prescribed amount of provisions, in such a way that, after giving alms, there will remain enough food for him and his family for at least 24 hours.

However, there is no obligation of these alms on the unborn fetus, unless the parents or the guardian wants to give on its behalf voluntary alms. The Leader of the Faithful, Umar (raa), gave for the unborn.

Thus, it is incumbent on every able believer to give for himself, and for those that he is responsible for; wife and children, and next of kin if they cannot give for themselves. If they can give, it is better that they do so, because every believer is commanded to do so.

In the event that the person does not possess the amount, alms-giving is not mandatory. But, if he possesses half of the amount, it should be given. Allah (SWT) states: "So fear Allah as much as you can..." (Al-Qur'an 64:16) And the Messenger of Allah said: "If I command you with something, do it as much as you can." (Agreed upon).

Spiritual Reasons For These Alms

The wisdom behind this obligation is, among other things, to extend a benevolent helping hand to needy Muslims so that they will not have to beg from their fellow wealthier believers on this happiest occasion of the year in a Muslim's life — Ramadan fast culminates with the festivity of Eid Prayer.

On the other hand, it helps the faster cleanse his fast from any shortcoming, or un-Islamic act during Ramadan. It is also to express gratitude to Allah for helping the servant live through another Ramadan. In a hadith reported by Ibn Abbas (raa) he said: "The Messenger of Allah (saas) has mandated the obligation of fast-breaking alms as a cleanser of the faster from (what one may have done) mistakes or obscene acts, and to provide for the poor. Whoever gives it before Eid prayer, it is an accepted alms, but whoever gives it after Eid prayer, it is only a charity like any ordinary charity." (Abu Dawud)

What Should Be Given?

Unlike regular Zakaat, the item recommended for giving is foodstuff: dates, wheat, barley, rice, oats, raisins, or any food stuff that can be stored naturally. Indeed, any type of food that is a staple in a given region of the vast Muslim world will do. If the staple is rice, you give rice, if it is dates or raisins, you give dates and raisins, etc.

In a hadith related by Bukhari and Muslim, by the way of Abdullah bin Umar (raa), he said: "The Messenger of Allah has established the fast-breaking alms of Ramadan, *sa'a*, a beaker of dates, or a beaker of barley, and barley was then part of our food." This hadith has been corroborated by another report by Abu Sa'eed Al-Khudri (raa) who said: "We used to give during the time of the Messenger a *sa'a*, a beaker of food, and our food was barley, raisins, dry milk, and dates." (Bukhari)

Thus, for these alms, items like cloth, cash money or currency, furniture, dishes and general goods are not accepted by Allah.

A sa'a (beaker) equivalent will not do. In so much as nothing else will substitute for these alms as a medium of giving, the monetary equivalent of the cost of a staple food will not be acceptable. For giving money, instead of food, is contrary to what the Messenger (saas) commanded. In a hadith, related by the mother of the believers, 'Aisha (raa) the Prophet (saas) said: "He who innovates something in this matter of ours, that is not of it, will have it rejected." (Bukhari and Muslim)

In Muslim's report of the hadith, the Messenger (saas) said: "He who does an act which our matter is not (in agreement) with will have it rejected." According to these two citations, to give money as Zakaatul-Fitr is an innovation and not proper, nor is it in accord with the prescribed worship, *'ebadah*. Alms giving is an act of worship, prescribed for a special item, food at a special time, i.e., before Eid prayer. The opinion of giving a monetary equivalent is reported from Imam Abu Hanifah (raa) who did not really have a proof, except *ijtihad*. There is no ijtihad where there is a text. After all, all the Imams, including Imam Abu Hanifa, Imama Shafie, Imam Malik, and Imam Ahmad said:

"If they say something that contradicts the established command of the Messenger of Allah, their saying should be discarded." (Raful Malam An Aimahtul Aalaam)

Sometimes the advocates of money as a substitute for food make us think there was no money during the time of the Prophet. To the contrary, there was money currency known as *"dirham"* and *"dinaar."* Giving monetary equivalents as fast-breaking alms relegates this act to a secret charity, rather than alms given as a religious ceremony *(Sha'eerah)*, which is to be observed publicly among the Muslims in a way that everybody in Muslim households, young and old, will participate in and bear witness to this extraordinary event of purchasing, weighing, and distributing food items among the needy faithful. This undoubtedly is one of the intents of the Lawgiver, a special cultural phenomenon unique to Islam and Muslims.

The evidence and wisdom behind giving food is more compelling than giving money. However, if the believer desires to help the needy more, giving money along with the prescribed food, is excellent and will be rewarded by Allah.

The Amount To be Given

As for the amount to be given, it is a *sa'a*, (a prophetic beaker) which is equal to about two kilos and forty grams. In pounds it is about five pounds per believer. If you want to know the prophetic *sa'a*, beaker, you weigh five pounds or two kilos and forty grams.

Put the weight in a beaker, jar or vessel and notice the level. You then use that as your *sa'a* to weigh the rest of your alms.

Better yet, a *sa'a*, can be purchased at a very reasonable price all over the Muslim world; if you happen to be in Makkah for Hajj or 'Umrah, you may purchase one or have someone who goes there to purchase it for you.

Time of Zakaatul-Fitr

Giving these alms is mandatory after sunset on the eve of *Eidul-Fitr*. If a Muslim expires seconds before sunset, it is not mandatory for his next of kin to give on his behalf. But if he expires seconds after sunset, alms should be given on his behalf. So is the case of the newly born.

As for the time it should be given, there are two time periods: The best and optional times. The best time is the morning of *Eidul-Fitr* before prayer. In a Hadith related by Ibn 'Umar (raa), "The Messenger of Allah (saas) commanded the Muslims to give alms when fast-breaking people leave for Eid prayer." (Muslim and others)

In his commentary on the following verse, Ibn 'Uyainah said: "But those will prosper who purify them (give alms) and glorify the name of their guardian Lord and pray."

He said: the word *"tazakka,"* purify or giving alms, comes before the word *"Salla,"* prayer. This is why it is better to delay

Eidul-Fitr prayer so that the believers will have enough time to give their alms.

The optional time to give alms is one or two days before Eid, that is on the 28th and 29th day of Ramadan. Legally, you have these three days to give your alms. But it should not be delayed past Eid prayer. In that case, *Zakaatul-Fitr* is not valid unless there is a reason, as mentioned earlier in the Hadith of Ibn Abbas (raa).

But if there is a compelling reason, such as Eid occurring in a place where there is no food to be purchased, or the food is bought, but there is no one to receive it, or the news about Eid comes late in the morning and one does not have enough time to buy the alms, or he depends on someone to give his Zakaat on his behalf, and the person forgets. In these instances, the alms can be given after Eid because of the valid excuse.

The alms should reach its recipients before Eid prayer, not after. The beneficiaries should physically have it in their possession. If you intend to give alms to someone and he cannot be found, it should be given to someone else, so that you do not miss the time.

Place In Which Alms Should Be Given

The alms should be given at the place where the Ramadan ends for the faster, home or abroad. If you happen to be in Makkah, Medina or Cairo you give it to the needy Muslims of that area.

If there are more poor Muslims in a given place, or there is no one who deserves the alms in your area, or you do not know anyone, you may deputize someone to give it on your behalf in a different country where Muslims are in need.

The Recipients of the Alms

The recipients of this Zakaat are the needy Muslims and those in debt. They should be given according to their needs. In a hadith by Ibn Umar (raa) the Prophet said: "Make them self sufficient on this day…" *(Dar Qutni)* It may be given to more than one needy person, or all may be given to one person.

REDEMPTION OF RAMADAN

When a faster misses a day or days due to valid reasons mentioned previously, they should be redeemed after Ramadan. The redemption is mandatory, not immediately but delayed mandatory, known as *"wajib'alt-Tarakhi."* Although by this jurisprudent principle, there is a period of eleven months to complete your Ramadan, it is preferred to make up these missed days as soon as possible, for Allah (SWT) says: "...Then strive together (as in a race) towards all that is good..." *(Al-Qur'an, 2:148)*.

This verse indicates hastening to offer deeds is preferred for that is the in the spirit of completing your Ramadan, and absolving the faster of the liability of unfasted days, rather than have it drag on for eleven months. After all, there is a possibility of death and missing the days altogether, as a result.

If there is reason to delay the redemption, it must not be delayed later than before the next Ramadan, or no later then the number of days he missed before the next Ramadan. If he missed five days, they should be redeemed not later than five days before the next Ramadan.

In an authenticated hadith attributed to 'Aishah (raa), she was accostumed to makeing up missed days in the month of *Sha'aban*, a month before Ramadan. If you miss more than one day you have the option to make them up consecutively or separately. Allah (SWT) states: "Fasting is for a fixed number of days. But if any of you is ill or on a journey, the missed number (of days) should be redeemed from days later...." *(Al-Qur'an, 2:187)* Thus, one who is ill or travels during Ramadan and does not fast, should fast days later to cover the ones missed, either in a group, all five days together, observed from Monday through Friday, or spread the five days over a whole month.

In a hadith related by Ibn 'Umar (raa), the Messenger of Allah said, referring to the redeeming of missed Ramadan fasts: "If he pleases, he redeems separately or consecutively." (Dar-Qutni)

No one should delay the making up of his missed days until next Ramadan, unless there is a valid reason. In this event, one should fast the present Ramadan, then make up the days missed in the previous Ramadan as soon as possible before the next Ramadan.

FASTING ON BEHALF OF THE DECEASED

We know that when a person who dies did not make Salaat, no one should pray on his behalf, nor should anyone fast on behalf of a person who could not observe fast. But if an able person dies before he completes Ramadan, no one need fast on his behalf, according to the majority of the scholars, but his next of kin should expiate on his behalf by feeding one person for each of the remaining days of Ramadan.

No fasting is mandatory on the deceased's family if he dies in the middle of Ramadan.

According to others, if the person dies before completing the missed days or before he makes up his oath *(nadhir)* the fast becomes mandatory and his or her next of kin must fast to make and expiate on his behalf. They cited a hadith reported by many, including Ahmed, Bukhari and Muslim in which the Messenger of Allah, said as reported by his wife, 'Aishah (raa): "He who dies while there is upon him the obligation of fast, his next of kin (*"Wali"*), fast on his behalf."

In another report by Ibn Abbas (raa), he said: "A man came to the Messenger of Allah and asked him, Oh Messenger of Allah, my mother passed away and upon her is the obligation of fast, should I make it up?' The Prophet (saas) responded: If your mother was indebted, would you pay back her debt?' He said, Yes.' The Prophet (saas), then said, the debt of Allah is worthy of paying.' These authenticated citations are evidence that redeeming the fast, interrupted by death, became mandatory upon the relatives of the deceased."

MUSLIMS NEAR THE NORTH OR SOUTH POLE

Muslims who live close to the North or South Pole, where there are long nights expanding over six months, or where the days expand over six months respectfully, should fast by using the time zone of the country nearest to them.

THE NIGHT OF POWER

Part of the significance of the Night of Power, has been previously mentioned. Let's analyze this topic with commentary, *(tafseer)* on chapter 97 of Al-Qur'an, *Al-Qadr* (the Night of Power).

Al-Qadr

This chapter *(surah)* was revealed in Makkah, and its basic theme is honoring the revelation of this blessed book, the Holy Quran. The Night of Power or honor is a special gift only to the community (Ummah) of Islam. The night is one which even the angels in the heavens see as worthy of witnessing. The night is so rich with holiness, as the night when good deeds are returned, and is equal to a thousand months in the sight of Allah.

Occasion Of Revelation

In a report by Abi Hatim and Al-Wahidi, by way of Mujahid, the Messenger (saas) mentioned that there was a man among the Israelites who devoted his life to the cause of Allah for a thousand months. The companions were amazed and impressed, but were saddened because they knew there would be no way that they could reach this status of devotion. So Allah (SWT) revealed this surah to inform them that He had just blessed this Ummah with the Night of Honor, which is equal to a thousand months.

"We have indeed revealed it, (Al-Qur'an) in the Night of Power." *(Al-Qur'an 97:1)*

There are several points pertaining to the meaning of this verse:

The meaning and the use of the pronoun "We" is a style in Al-Qur'an that when the Creator (SWT) is mentioned as a pronoun, He is referred to by either "We" or "I," as is evidenced in this surah. Elsewhere He said, "Behold, thy Lord said to the angels: I will create a vicegerent..." *(Al-Qur'an, 2:30)*. There is no problem when Allah uses the pronoun "I" to refer to His Exalted Self, but when he uses "We" the explanation becomes warranted because it cannot be perceived to indicate plural. There is unanimity among the scholars that "We" indicates respect and exaltation for the Creator and Cherisher of all the worlds, Whose greatness is incomprehensibly vast and beyond our imagination.

Or, it is referring to Allah (SWT) and the angels who carry out his words to one and all in every level of His dominion. It cannot mean plural, or more than One Allah, for that would necessitate dropping in ranks, the absoluteness, and the powers of each competing deity. If each is capable of being absolute, each would have been independent from the other and the idea that each deity can be independent from the other, is evidence that none is absolute. This is inconceivable of Allah (SWT) therefore, "We" cannot mean anything but respect and exaltation of the One and Only.

"...Have Indeed Revealed It In the Night of Power"
(Al-Qur'an 97:1)

There is again unanimity among the commentators that "it" refers to *Al-Qur'an*, meaning "We revealed" *Al-Qur'an* in the Night of Power. He (SWT) did not mention *Al-Qur'an* explicitly because to refer to *Al-Qur'an* by the pronoun implies a certain divine uniqueness of this book, as well as greatness and honor that may not be attained if the word *Al-Qur'an* was used instead. First, it ascribed the revelation of *Al-Qur'an* to Himself, and not to anyone else. Second, referring to *Al-Qur'an* by pronoun is an indication that the revelation of this book was not a secret that no one knew about. Its revelation was an event widely known to all during the time of Muhammad (saas) and after, guarding against anyone who may like to challenge it or claim any honor of teaching Muhammad (saas) *Al-Qur'an*. Third, the statement also meant to honor and memorialize the time period in which *Al-Qur'an* was revealed.

By revealing *Al-Qur'an* in the Night of Power, Allah (SWT) inaugurated or started its revelation for the beginning of the prophethood *('Bi'ethah)*, and the Prophet's mission of *Al-Islam* began in the month of Ramadan on that Night. *Al-Qur'an* was not revealed in one night; it was revealed over the course of 23 years. Ibn Abbas (raa) said: The whole Quran was revealed to the lower heavens from the protective slate *(Lauhu Mahfuz)* on the Night of Power, then from there to the earth in the course of 23 years.

The word power, *Al-Qadr*, has several implications and meanings, but we cover only those implications which are relevant to the issues here.

Qadr implies having power over something, as in the case of the Creator over the creation. Allah's (SWT) excellence is *Al-Qadr*, capable, omnipotent, almighty, all powerful. It also implies excellence and high esteem, and as for this Night of Power, it is highly esteemed and regarded. For this night is equal to over 80 years in the sight of Allah (SWT).

It also implies to maintain, appoint, assign or decree an order. Thus, in the Night of Power, Allah (SWT) proclaims to the angels His commands and orders in regards to the affairs of the universe. From this meaning is derived the concept of *Al-Qada Wa Qadar*, the fifth article of faith, that Allah has decreed or preordained or, in other words, has full knowledge of all that the human being will do with his free will. A man's decision to act freely in good conscience or bad conscience is all known to Allah (SWT), past, present and future.

Qadr also implies measurement, that is all the events of the year will occur in accordance to the exact measurement of what is in the knowledge of Allah, Who states: "Verily, all things have We created in proportion and measure." *(Al-Qur'an, 54:49)*

Why the name, the Night of Power?

As mentioned above, it is the night of Taqdeer, meaning the one in which Allah (SWT) announces to the angels His already decreed commands, rules, events, etc., for the coming calendar year, from the present Night of Power to the next Night of Power. Allah (SWT) states:

"We sent it down during a blessed night; We forever wish to warn (against evil). In that (night) is made distinct every affair of wisdom." *(Al-Qur'an, 44:3-4)*

It should be known that most scholars believe Allah's commands and rules are not made on that night. It has already been decreed in the eternity what is known to Allah, but that knowledge is not known to anyone, including the angels, until He announces it to the angels on that night so that they will record it on the protective slate and carry it at his command.

This is also the night of honor and prestige which may be awarded to the servant who devotes himself to special deeds, or to the deeds themselves for the higher value they contain on that night.

The Night Is Concealed

Allah (SWT) in His mercy, has concealed the Night of Power from us for the following reasons: The problems pertaining to an exact night on which the honors are attained are not unique with this Night. It seems that Allah conceals many things. He conceals his pleasure from us in all our good deeds so that we will strive in all of them. He conceals His wrath from us in all of the sins we commit so that we will avoid them all. He conceals His most beloved servants (*'awliya*) so that we will respect all the believers. He has concealed the time of His acceptance of our supplications so that we will strive in all our supplications. He concealed his greatest name, so that we mention all His names. He has concealed the time of death so that we will be conscious of Him and our deeds all the time. He has concealed the exact date of the Night of Power so that we would double our efforts in the whole month of Ramadan, or at least in the last ten days.

He has concealed it also to test the serious and the non-serious. The seriously interested person will search for the night late and in the early hours until he or she attains it, regardless of the hardship.

Where Is The Night?

The majority of the scholars who agreed that the night occurs in the month of Ramadan, disagreed on the exact night. Some said it comes on the first day of Ramadan. Others said it is on the seventh; while others say it is on the 19th night. All these opinions are not built on sound proof. There is evidence that the night comes on the last ten days of Ramadan, specifically on the odd numbered nights. In a report by Bukhari, the Messenger of Allah (saas) said: "Seek it on the odd nights of the last ten days of Ramadan."

In a hadith by Ibn Umar (raa), some men among the companions saw the night in a dream occurring in the last seven nights. Responding to this, the Messenger of Allah (saas) told them, "I see your dreams coincide on the last seven, whoever wants to seek it should do so in the last seven." (Agreed upon)

In Muslim's report, the Prophet (saas) said, "Seek the night in the last ten days, and if any of you is weak, or can't observe it, he should not miss the remaining seven days." In Hadith by Ubayy bin Ka'ab (raa), he said: "By Allah, I know which night it is. It is the night the Messenger commanded us to observe, the night of the 27th." (Ahmed/Tirmidhi)

Analyzing all these citations indicates still no one knows for sure which night is the Night of Power, at least in a given year. It seems that the night shifts and rotates to different nights from one year to another. It may occur on the 27th in one year, while the next year it will be on the 25th, while on the following year it will be occurring on the 29th, etc. There is an indication to this in hadith by Bukhari, when the Messenger of Allah (saas) states: "Seek it on the twenty-ninth; it may be on the twenty-seventh, or on the twenty-fifth." Imam Ibn Hajr, in his book, "*Fathul Bari,*" the commentary of the Book of Bukhari, said: "I accept the ruling that the night occurs on the odd nights of the last ten days of Ramadan, namely the twenty-first, twenty-third, twenty-fifth, twenty-seventh and or twenty-ninth."

Seeking The Night

It is recommended to seek the night and spend it diligently in devotion, including night Sunnah prayers *(Tahajjud)*, recitation of *Al-Qur'an* and supplications. In a hadith related by Abu Hurairah (raa), the Messenger of Allah (saas) said: "He who spends the night in prayer on the Night of Power, as a sign of His faith, and seeking rewards from Allah, his previous sins will be forgiven." (Bukhari/Muslim) This citation indicates that regardless of whether a person knows the night or not, Allah will grant him forgiveness for previous shortcomings.

"And what will explain to thee what the Night of Power is?; The Night of Power is better than a thousand months." (Al-Qur'an 97:2–3)

Allah (SWT) is emphasizing by putting the second verse in question form. The answer being no one knows, or comprehends, the awesomeness and the depth of honor of the night. As if to say whatever merits Allah informs you about the night is just nothing compared to the things you have no idea about. Nonetheless, He mentions three honors in the credit of the night: 1. "The Night is better than a thousand months." 2. "Therein, come down the angels..." and 3. "Peace!"

The Night of Power is better than a thousand months. This indicates that acts of worship such as prayer, charity, and recitation done on this night are better in reward than the same act done on other nights. The rewards *(thawaab)* are being multiplied several-fold.

Imam Malik reported that the Messenger of Allah (saas) was shown the long life span of people of previous nations, so the Prophet bemoaned the shortness of the life span of the Ummah, fearing that they might not be able to save many good deeds for the Hereafter. Therefore, Allah gave him the Night of Power to compensate for their lack of longevity. Hence, the devoted believer has a chance of adding 80 something years of worship to his life on the Night of Power. You see, for instance, if you worship Allah on this night every year for 65 years, by multiplying 65 by

80, you would have lived for 5,200 years, or achieved the reward of a person who lived that long.

You can see why the devotions were highly encouraged by the Prophet. Indeed, you can achieve the honor of the Night of Power if you so wish by spending the odd nights of the last ten days in acts of worship.

"Therein, come down the angels and the Spirit by Allah's permission, on every errand." (Al-Qur'an 97:4)

This is far from the earlier cry of the angels who, when Allah told them, "...I will create a vicegerent on earth," they said, "Will you place therein one who will make mischief therein and shed blood?..." (Al-Qur'an, 2:30)

You see, when the angels first looked at our spirit with its traits of mischief, vanity and desires, and the rages of anger, they, the embodiment of all that is good, did not like us at all. That explains their response in the above verse. So is the case with parents, when they first conceptualize the shape of the offspring, semen and congealed blood; they do not like it. They will even wash their hands, clothes and everything that this substance touches, a gruesome thing. They may even think about aborting the baby in the beginning.

But after the baby is being fashioned in the most beautiful shape and they feel the movement of life, they change from dislike to caring love.

That is seemingly what happened to the angels. When they saw in us this beautiful spirit of knowing the Creator, and worshipping Allah alone, they changed from dislike to complete love, and cannot wait for another Night of Power to come down so they can pray for us. Allah states: "...And they implore forgiveness for those who believe..." (Al-Qur'an, 40:7)

He used the form *(tanazzal)* "They come," to indicate that the angels descend on the Night of Power, group after group; some coming down to earth while others ascend into the heaven. This heavenly, angelic organized traffic of good will continues until the break of dawn.

·As for the reasons why they come, there are several explanations including: (1) they descend to witness how we worship and obey Allah, and (2) to show their deep love for the believers. This is why they seek permission from Allah to come and meet us. This is a once-a-year opportunity they do not like to miss. (3) Allah promised the believers that in the hereafter, angels will approach them with greetings: "...And the angels shall enter into them from every gate (with the salutation): Peace be unto you for that you persevered in patience..." *(Al-Qur'an, 13:23–24)*

Now, if you preoccupy yourself with worship of Allah, the angels will descend on you with salutations. (4) Allah (SWT) singles out this night with honors on the earth so the angels can come down and increase their rewards, and as a means to encourage the human race to worship. (5) Realization that the angels are around is encouragement for the servants to devote more time to good deeds as a man will work harder when a foreman is present.

"... And the Spirit..." (Al-Qur'an 97:4)

There are several explanations for the meaning of the Spirit: (1) The Spirit is comprised of groups of special angels who are seen only on the Night of Power; (2) it is referring to *Al-Qur'an*, as Allah (SWT) stated: "And thus have We, by Our command sent inspiration (spirit) to thee..." *(Al-Qur'an 42:52)*, (3) This is a reference to Angel Jibreel, as this is a special honor to Jibreel who has been mentioned twice in the Suurah, first with other angels, and separately as the spirit of Allah (SWT) as the Quran says: "Verily this is a revelation from the Lord of the Worlds. With it came down the spirit of faith and truth." *(Al-Qur'an, 26:192–193)* Thus the correct explanation of the spirit, *Ruuh*, is Jibreel in this verse to indicate the angels will be on one side and Jibreel on the other, while they were descending.

"...By Allahs permission..."

This indicates the angels extend a request to come to meet the believers, and to underscore the fact that angels are infallible; they do not make a move without explicit permission from their Lord. Allah (SWT) states: "They speak not before He speaks, and they act (in all things) by His command." *(Al-Qur'an, 21:27)* "(The angels say) We descend not but by command of thy Lord..." *(Al-Qur'an 19:64)*

"(Their) Lord." It indicates honor for the angels. It is as if Allah (SWT) is saying "They are for Me and I am for them." Similarly, Allah (SWT) said regarding us: "Verily your Lord is Allah Who created the heavens and the earth in six days..." *(Al-Qur'an, 10:3)* And regarding Prophet Muhammad (saas) Allah said: "Behold, your Lord said to the angels..." *(Al-Qur'an, 2:30)*

It has been reported that when Prophet David was terminally ill, he asked Allah to be for his son Solomon, as He was for him.

Allah (SWT) replied, saying: "Tell Solomon to be for Me as you are for Me." *(Al-Qur'an 2:30)*

"... On every errand..."

This indicates the angels and the Spirit descend for different purposes: some come down for prostration, some for bowing, and others for supplications for the believers and salutations. Or they come down carrying with them the proclamations of the coming year.

5. *"Peace!..." (Al-Quran 97:5)*

There are several explanations to this verse: (1) The whole Night of Power, from sunset to the break of dawn, will be spent by the angels in salutation. (2) The purpose is to describe the night with peace because of the salutation from the angels. That is very important, because when seven angels visited Prophet Ibrahim (saas) and saluted him, he was very happy, and when Nimrod threw him in the fire, it turned ice-cold when the angels saluted him. (3) This is a wish of safety and peace from all evil and harmful things, or the angels will only bring on this night, good things!

"... Until the rise of morn." (Al-Qur'an 97:5)

All the honor, blessings and peace of the Night of Power will continue in every second of the night until Fajr. Allah (SWT) is the Best Knower.

ACHIEVING THE ESSENCE OF OBEDIENCE

From the outset, for an act or deed to be considered a proper worship, 'ebadah, it must contain two things: **(1)** Sincerity *(Ikhlas)*. It must be offered simply for the sole purpose of pleasing Allah (SWT) and seeking His pleasure. Allah, said: "And they have been commanded no more than this, to worship Allah offering Him sincere devotion..." *(Al-Qur'an 98:5)*. **(2)** It must be done in accordance with the commands of Allah (SWT) and the practice of the Messenger of Allah (saas); that is what is called obedience *(mutaaba'ah)*. Allah (SWT) states: "Say: if you do love Allah, follow me, Allah will love you and forgive you your sins. For Allah is oft Forgiving, Most Merciful." *(Al-Qur'an 3:31)*

This verse indicates whoever claims to love Allah without following the commands of the Messenger, his claims are lies. To be a true lover of Allah one has to obey, and his deeds must mirror those of the Messenger of Allah (saas). This is why many scholars call this verse the verse of trial, because we have been tried to see whether we will obey or not. The Messenger said: "Whoever does a deed without our command, it will be rejected." (Muslim/Bukhari) To achieve the essence of obedience, six points must be considered. I call them the essence of obedience.

(1) **REASON** *(SABABB)*,

(2) **METHOD** *(KAYFIYYAH)*,

(3) **KIND** *(JINS)*,

(4) **AMOUNT** *(QADAR)*,

(5) **PLACE** *(MAKAAN)*, and

(6) **TIME** *(ZAMAAN)*.

The acts of worship are inclusive in one or more of these six essences:

Reason *(Sababb)*

If you worship Allah for a reason, you must make sure the reason is given or pointed out to you by Allah (SWT) or the Messenger of Allah (saas). It must not be a reason rationalized by you, or someone else for you. Hence, regular virtuous acts of Salaat, Fasting, or *dhikir* will be considered invalid if done for the wrong reasons. For instance, in certain parts of the Muslim world, some Muslims gather together in the month of Rajab to commemorate *"Al-Isra Wal mi'eraj,"* the night journey Prophet Muhammad (saas) took from Makkah to Jerusalem, and from there his ascension to the heavens. This story is in _Suurah 17 in Al-Qur'an._ During this celebration, participants offer Salaat, _dhikir, sadaqah_ as reason, etc. This annual celebration cannot be considered valid because the reason given is not sanctioned by Allah (SWT) or His Messenger.

The Islamic term for acts like these is _Bid'ah,_ or innovation. For the question will be, did Allah (SWT) or His Prophet (saas) command us to celebrate _'Al-Isra'?_ There is no proof anywhere to be found. Did the Messenger of Allah (saas) know this was a good reason for celebration? If you say he did not know, you have accused him of ignorance. If you say he did know, but did not inform us, you are accusing him of cheating, and the Messenger of Allah (saas) is above that. Indeed, Allah (SWT) has described him as being merciful to the believers, and with a keen interest in informing the believers about everything that is good. After all, there is a disagreement among the learned scholars about the month in which "Isra" took place. The most accepted opinion is that it was in Rabee'ul Awwal.

One may ask how would acts of charity, prayer and _dhikir_ be labeled, _bid'ah?_ You see, these acts in and of themselves are not innovation. What is innovation is offering them with unsanctioned reason. Another example, there are certain sufi orders who make _dhikir,_ believing that at a certain number the Messenger of Allah (saas) will attend this gathering and bless them. Unfortunately, these people will get nothing from their efforts because of wrong, unsanctioned reasoning.

Method _(Kayfiyyah)_

This Ummah has been blessed in that Allah (SWT) did not let it wander in the dark as to how to worship Him, or what he liked or disliked of the worship. The methods _(kayfiyyah)_ of acts of worship have been thoroughly described by Allah, and His Messenger. He says: "(We sent them) with Clear Signs and Books of divine prophecies, and We have sent down unto thee (also) the Message, that you mayest explain clearly to people what is sent for them, and that they may give thought." _(Al-Qur'an, 16:44)_

Also, He (SWT) says: "...Nothing have we omitted from the Book..." _(Al-Qur'an, 6:38)_ These two verses indicate if you are looking for the basis for any act, it must be found in Al-Qur'an. If the explanation in _Al-Qur'an_ is not clear enough, the Prophet (SWT) will explain it in his authenticated Sunnah. It follows then that every conceivable act of _ebadah_ has been detailed in Islamic sources. You are not left to fend for yourself. Thus, no one has the right to make a method, *kayfiyyah,* of *ebadah* on his own, nor should he or she allow anyone else to do it for him, no matter how well versed or respected an individual may be. He may be a Companion, a follower of a Companion, an Imam or a saint.

For instance, if a Muslim decides to make wudu, ablution, before Salaat, and begins by washing his feet, then face, arms, head, ears, and winds up with his nose, a complete wudu in terms of thoroughness and amount of washing has been done. But that Wudu is not valid for prayer, because the method, *(kayfiyyah)* is not correct because in the method of wudu, sequence *(muwaalat)* is an important element. Disregarding sequence makes the wudu invalid. Also, let us say a believer thinks the method of cleanliness *(taharah)* is bathing. So he neglects wudu altogether, thinking he has just finished bathing. His Salaat will not be valid because the only method for cleanliness before Salat is wudu. Allah (SWT) said: "O you who believe! When you prepare for prayer, wash you face and your hands (and arms) to the elbows, rub your heads (with water), and wash your feet to the ankles..." *(Al-Qur'an, 5:7)*

Kind *(Jins)*

The kind, *jins,* of a thing or an act must be in accordance with what Allah (SWT) or the Prophet (saas) prescribed. For instance, one of the annual events during the time of *'Eidul-Adhah* is sacrifice of cattle *(udhiyah).* By cattle is meant a camel, cow, lamb and/or a goat. If a believer decides to sacrifice the best *(udhiyah)* he has for Allah (SWT) and he happens to have a thoroughbred horse worth thousands of dollars and a sheep worth only 85 dollars, and if he decides to sacrifice the horse instead of the sheep, his sacrifice will not be accepted. Although the sacrifice was exceedingly expensive, the horse is not what is asked of him as a sacrifice. It is cattle that he is commanded to sacrifice.

In another example, on the eve of *'Eidul-Fitr,* the Lawgiver prescribes food as the medium of *Zakaatul-Fitr* (fast-breaking charity) after Ramadan. If an individual decides to give the monetary equivalent, the Zakaat will not be valid because the Lawgiver's explicit command is food not money.

Amount *(Qadar)*

The amount and number, *qadar,* for certain acts of worship have already been established by the Lawgiver, such as five times daily prayers, two-and-a-half percent for Zakaat, *tawaaf* (circumambulation) during Hajj or Umrah, fasting during Ramadan, etc. If the amount is four, two or three, that is what it should be, no more no less. For instance, if a believer decides to make *Zuhr* prayer five raka'ats instead of four, he may have made them in the most excellent way, but five raka'ats for Zuhr prayer is invalid because the prescribed amount of raka'ats for Zuhr is four. After all, *Maghrib* prayer is the only odd numbered daily prayer, not Zuhr. Similarly, nobody has a right to prescribe for himself or for anyone else the amount and number of *dhikirs* (remembrance of Allah) and *tasbeeh* (glorification of Allah) without first having the bases for it in Al-Qur'an and or Sunnah.

Place *(Makaan)*

The place, *makaan,* for the act of worship to take place must be established by the Lawgiver. No one can concoct a holy place for himself or others without approval from the Lawgiver. For instance, if a believer decides to make *I'etikaaf,* (the retreat in the Masjid for the sake of worship) in the last ten days of Ramadan, but makes it in his house instead of the Masjid, his I'etikaaf will not be valid because the only place for I'etikaaf is the Masjid. Allah (SWT) said: *"...While you are in retreat in the Masjid..."* *(Al-Qur'an, 2:187)* So is the case if a person decides to make *tawaaf* (circumambulation) around a building instead of Ka'abah, or stand on a mountain other than the plane of 'Arafah, the tawaaf and standing will not be valid.

Time *(Zamaan)*

The time, *zamaan,* for every act has already been prescribed. For instance, if a believer decides to fast Ramadan in the month of December because it is shorter and a cooler month instead of the ninth lunar month, Ramadan, his or her fasting will not be valid because of the wrong time. Similarly, if he decides to stand on the plain of 'Arafah, but he did so on the tenth day of Dhul-Hijjah, his standing will be like standing on any plain at any time, and religiously valueless.

Therefore, any act that does not correspond with these six reasons, method, kind, amount, place, and time will be labeled an innovation, *bid'ah*, because Allah says: "...This day have I completed your religion for you, completed my favor upon you, and have chosen for you Islam as your religion." *(Al-Qur'an, 5:4)*

This verse indicates the religion of Islam is complete and has been perfected. Allah (SWT) uses two words to underscore this fact. *Akmaltu*, from the root word *"kamula"* (complete, perfect), and *atmantu* from the root word, *"tamma,"* (completed, finished, perfected and filled up). If the cap is full, can you add anything to it? If you do it will spill, and you may not know whether it is the orginal that spills or the added. That spill is the *bid'ah*. Allah (SWT) is the best knower.

WHAT CONSTITUTES INNOVATION *(BID'AH)?*

When we speak of innovation in Islam, we are speaking strictly of religious acts and deeds. In a hadith the Messenger of Allah stated: "He who innovates something in this matter of ours that is not of it will have it rejected." (Bukhari/ Muslim) In another report he said: "He who does an act which our matter is not (in agreement) with will have it rejected." (Muslim) These citations indicate what the Messenger meant by innovation as a strictly religious act. So no act is labeled innovation *(bid'ah)* unless it has been promoted or introduced as a religion. If an act or deed is non-religious it is not considered innovation. The material and physical products can not de called bid'ah. For instance, the technical innovations or developments in the mode of transportation from horses and camels to cars and jet planes are not called innovations. Indeed, Islam applauds loudly any technical development that makes the acts of 'ebadah easy and convenient. The technical developments are part of the custodianship or stewardship *(khilaafaship)* that man has been endowed with. In other words the theological innovations are illegal whereas the technical innovations are not. After all Allah (SWT) states:

''And (he has created) horses, mules and donkeys, for you to ride and use for show and He will yet create things of which ye have no knowledge." (Al-Qur'an, 16: 8)

Allah in the verse has prophesied the creation of advanced vehicles from a simple car to orient express to the most sophisticated machinery, engine, and rockets. The lightning speed with which we advanced in computers, chips, lazars, satellites, fabric, technology etc., are highly honored as they may lead some to the realization of the power of Almighty Allah.

RAMADAN NIGHTLY PRAYER *(TARAWEEH)*

Allah (SWT) has mandated to His servants acts of worship and made them of various kinds so as to provide them with means to pick and choose, and that they will not be bored with one act. Thus, we seek nearness to Him, through mandatory and non-mandatory deeds. Among the non-mandatory deeds, or Sunnahs, is the establishment of night time prayers *(salatul lail)*, and Allah has praised those who observe them.

"Those who spend the night in adoration of their Lord, prostrate and standing." *(Al-Qur'an 25:64)*

"Their limbs do forsake their beds of sleep, the while they call on their Lord in fear and hope and they spend (in charity) out of the sustenance which we have bestowed on them."*(Al-Qur'an 32:16)*

These two verses indicate the basis for nightly prayer in *Al-Qur'an* and the good return awaiting those who observe it. In a hadith, the Messenger of Allah (saas) says: "The best prayer after the obligatory ones is the night prayer." (Muslim)

Elsewhere he says: "O people! Disseminate the salutations of peace *As-Salaam 'Alaikum*; feed the needy food, and join the blood ties among the next of kin, and observe night prayer while people are at sleep, you will enter paradise peacefully." (Tirmidhi)

One of the night prayers, is *Witr*, the odd numbered bedtime prayer. It should be the last prayer said before retiring at night. The minimum Witr is one *rak'ah* and the maximum is eleven raka'ats. The Prophet (saas) said: "Whoever wants to pray Witr with one raka'ah should do it and whoever wants to pray *Witr* with three raka'ats should do it." (Abud Dawud/Nasa'e).

However, the Messenger of Allah (saas) was always consistent with eleven raka'ats for night prayers, according to his wife, 'Aishah (raa) who reported: "The Prophet never observed prayers after Isha (night obligatory prayer) and before Fajr (morning prayer), more than eleven raka'ats. He saluted after every two raka'ats, and he prayed Witr with one raka'at." (Jama'ah, except Tirmi'dhi)

In a different procedure, one may make four raka'ats, and salute, and continue with another four and salute, then he caps them with three raka'ats of Witr. 'Aishah (raa) reported: "The Prophet used to pray four raka'ats and one cannot describe their beauty, and their length, (he salutes) then makes another set of four raka'ats, one cannot describe their beauty and length, he then caps it with three raka'ats." (Agreed upon)

TARAWEEH

The Ramadan nightly prayer has a special merit over other nights. The Messenger of Allah said: "Whoever observes night prayer in Ramadan as an expression of his faith and to seek reward from Allah, his previous sins will be blotted out." (Muslim)

In this hadith, faith means faith in what Allah has promised the observers of night prayers. To seek reward means, the observer's intent is not for eye service or seeking special recognition from someone.

Taraweeh is derived from the Arabic root word, *raaha*, which means to rest, relax and use as recreation. It is so called because the believers used to prolong it. After every four *raka'ats* they would stop for rest and relaxation and resume until taraweeh was complete.

Taraweeh in Jamaa'ah

The Messenger of Allah (saas) was the first to establish the Sunnah of congregational, *jamaaah* prayer of taraweeh in the Masjid. Then he did not continue with the Sunnah for fear that it might be made mandatory on the Ummah in Ramadan, and they might not be able to do it. In the books of Bukhari and Muslim, 'Aishah (raa) has been reported as saying:

"The Messenger of Allah (saas) observed (Taraweh) prayer in the Masjid one night and people prayed with him. He repeated the following night and the number of participants grew. The companions congregated the third and fourth night, but the Messenger did not show up. In the morning he told them, "I saw what you did last night, but nothing prevented me from joining you except my fear that it might be made mandatory on you in Ramadan."

This hadith is a clear indication that the *Taraweeh* in congregation was not an innovation of 'Umar, the second Khalifah, despite his saying to the contrary. For it has been related that: "Umar bin Al-Khattab (raa) attended the Masjid at night in Ramadan and saw people praying individually in every corner of the Masjid with a few in groups. He did not like the sight a bit. 'Umar said, 'I thought it would be better to gather these under one Imam.' So, he combined them under 'Obayi bin Ka'ab and Tamimu Ad-Dari to alternate and lead the believers in eleven raka'ats of night prayer. The next day Umar was in the Masjid which was full with

Taraweh prayers. He was delighted. He said: Well, this is the best Bid'ah (innovation).'"

Umar's use of the word *bid'ah* in this report has been presented and unjustifiably cited as justification for concocting up various so called good innovations. In truth, the Khalifah 'Umar's act to gather the believers in Jam'ah is not *bed'ah*. For it was the Messenger of Allah himself who started *jama'ah* by praying in congregation the first and second day, then stopped only as he feared it would become mandatory. After his death, the fear of Taraweh becoming mandatory (Fard) was not only remote, it was impossible. With the death of the Prophet Muhammad (saas), there will be no more revelation to change any law or rule by abrogation.

Number of *Rakaaats* in *Taraweeh*

As for the number of raka'ats in Taraweeh and Witr, the worthy ancestor, *Salaf as-Saalih* disagreed on the amount of Raka'ats. These numbers are mentioned for raka'ats: 39, 29, 23, 19, 13, and 11 raka'ats. Of all the numbers mentioned, none is sounder than 11 raka'ats. 'Aishah (raa) was asked how was the prayer of the Prophet (saas)? She replied: "He did not pray in Ramadan or some other times more than eleven raka'ats." (Muslim/Bukhari)

However, there is nothing wrong with praying more than 11 raka'ats. Perhaps that is why different numbers are observed. The Prophet himself was asked about night prayer and he said: "It may be done in two raka'ats, and if anyone fears the appearance of morning, he should pray one raka'ah as a Witr for what he has already prayed." (Bukhari/Muslim)

As this hadith indicates, if a person is to pray individually at night, by daybreak he would have prayed one hundred and one raka'ats, or more.

In their desire to pray more raka'ats, some people make Taraweh in extreme speed. That is wrong, especially when the speed leads to a breach of certain rules of prayer. In that case, the prayer will not be valid. Similarly, it is undesirable for an Imam to pray with such speed whereby the followers will have difficulty observing the necessary deeds in Salaat.

Neglecting *Taraweeh*

No one should neglect Taraweh without a good reason, for it is part of physical and spiritual training, for its observation soon after Iftar insures timely and proper digestion of food. Besides, there are spiritual rewards awaiting the observers of this prayer. No one would like to leave the Masjid before the prayer is over.

Everybody should attend the Masjid prayers, including women, provided they are properly covered. The Messenger of Allah said: "Prevent not the women servants of Allah, from going to the houses (Masajid) of Allah." However, when they attend the Masjid they should wear no perfume, nor raise their voices, and or show their beauty. Allah (SWT) states: "...they should not display their beauty and ornaments except what (must ordinarily) appear thereof..." *(Al-Qur'an, 24:31)*

What ordinarily appears, refers to the outer garments, for when the Messenger (saas) commanded women to attend Eid prayer, Umm 'Atiyah (raa) said: "O Messenger of Allah, some of us do not have the outer garment *(jilbab)*. The Messenger of Allah told her to let a sister (who has more than one) give or loan her one to wear." (Agreed upon)

It is Sunnah that they pray behind the men in the rear lines. The Messenger has been reported as saying: "The best lines for men are the front lines and the worst lines for men are the rear lines. The best lines for women is the rear and the worst lines of women are the front line." (Muslim)

The women should leave the Masjid as soon as the Imam says: *As-Salamu 'Alaikum*. They should not delay without a valid reason. In a hadith by Umm Salmah, she said: "'When the Messenger of Allah (saas) saluted to end prayer, the women would stand up to leave and the Messenger would remain in his place for a while.' Umm Salmah (raa) said: 'Allah is the best knower, perhaps the Messenger did that so women would leave before men could overtake them.'" (Bukhari)

THE WISDOM BEHIND FASTING

There are reasons and wisdom behind every single act in Islam, no matter how small. In time we may know the wisdom behind some acts, and for others we may never know. *Salaat*, for instance, is a daily training for purifying the believer and reminding him that he is a member in a community of believers. Fasting, on the other hand, is an annual institution containing all conceivable attributes for human excellence. It is a training for the body and soul, a renewal of life, encouraging the spirit of sharing and giving. The following are some of the general benefits:

Self — Restraint *(Taqwaa)*

Allah (SWT) states: "O you who believe! Fasting is prescribed to you as it was prescribed to those before you that you may (learn) self restraint." *(Al-Qur'anan, 2:183)*

This verse indicates that the first lesson or wisdom to be gained in fasting, is self-restraint, (Taqwa) or the fear of Allah (SWT). That is to say, fasting instills in the heart the essence of consciousness of the Creator, moral courage both in secret and manifest, guiding the heart, the seat of emotion from spoilage and moral indecency.

It has been reported that Abdul Malik bin Al-Asma'e was in Makkah when Ramadan came, so he decided to leave for Taif to escape its heat. On the way, he met a Bedouin who told him that he was heading for Makkah. Abdul Malik asked him, "'Aren't you afraid of Makkan heat in Ramadan?' The Bedouin replied, 'It is from the heat (hellfire) I am running away (by heading to Makkah to worship).'"

Fasting instills *taqwaa*, fear of Allah, and does so by controlling two aspects of the human body, which are the root causes of human downfall, namely the stomach and the private parts. The human body is constructed with the need to please the two of them and, in the process, man transgresses the rights of others, fellow human beings, and the commandments of Allah are violated. Fasting is equivalent to life, because with the level of *taqwaa* being raised, the person avoids the sins which are detrimental to life itself.

Behavior Modification

One of the most important things fasting affords the observer is helping him control or change his or her habits, the reason being that human life is an embodiment of acquired habits. To change or control a habit is to wage a war on yourself. If *jihaad* is mandatory on every believer because it is the peak of the essence in Islam, and it entails changing habits, the fasting is the training ground for the inevitable that will occur. The believer cannot wage a war and hope to defeat an enemy if he or she cannot wage war against his soul. Thus, the faster is admitted to the compulsory training opened only in Ramadan, the learning in this school is mandatory and succeeding or scoring high is mandatory, otherwise it is like you never entered. The Prophet (saas) said: "Many a faster receives naught from his fast except the pain of hunger and thirst."

If he scores high the reward is guaranteed: "Three people's prayers are not rejected-among them—the faster, until he breaks." (Ibn Hiban) Now, does a Ramadan fast control ones habits? Simple, two of the most important habits are food and drink. An average person eats three meals a day, 21 meals a week. The way the fast is structured, with its basic and drastic alteration of eating habits, a faster takes light meals early in the morning and late in the evening. If the believer can control these two habits, food and drink, it will undoubtedly be easy for him to control other habits, including the habits of smoking, drug abuse and illicit sex. Do you not see that, if you can control your tongue, hands and all other parts of your body, it will be easy for you to apply the same training for the rest of the year.

Health Care

The benefits of fasting transcend guiding the faster from idle talk and indecent acts. It is a sentinel against disease, provided the faster follows the strict dietary rule: eat during fast-breaking and avoiding over-eating. Allah (SWT) states: "...Eat and drink, but waste not by excess, for Allah loves not wasters." (Al-Qur'an, 7:31)

A great deal of ailments originate from stomach indigestion. This is why the Messenger of Allah (saas) says: "The son of Adam will never fill a container with something worse and evil than his stomach. It will suffice him some morsels (food) that will keep him on his feet, otherwise, he should divide his stomach into three parts: one third for his food, the other for his drink and the other third for his breath." (Ibn Hibban)

This hadith indicates that the stomach is the origin of harmful bacteria. Even in the age of sophisticated machines, you can hardly find a machine so fragile but yet so remarkably durable and efficient like the stomach. This is the machine that receives food particles, processes and refines them, and distributes the products to different parts of the body. This is a lifelong operation. For the non-faster, the stomach will have no chance for rest. When the stomach is empty, as a result of fasting, it gets well-desired rest, to renew and rejuvenate its energy. With the fasting, the stomach is forced to go through a discharge whereby harmful residue are eliminated through perspiration as the body searches for food during fast.

During fast, the system of secretion is organized, and this in turn benefits the blood pressure, inhibiting hardening of the arteries. The heart and kidney functions are enhanced as the work load tapers off. The fast helps to correct the problem of obesity and diabetes. Doctors over the years have used fasting as a prescription for certain ailments.

There was a discussion between Ali Bin Husain bin Waquid (raa) and a Christian physician to the Khalifah, Haroon Ar-Rasheed, about Islam's outlook on the science of medicine and health care. The physician said to Ibn Waquid: "'There is not in your Book, *Al-Qur'an*, anything about medicine. For if *Al-Qur'an* is a book of science, what about this science? Aren't there two kinds of sciences: the science of the body and the science of the soul?' Ibn Waquid responded: 'Allah, the Most High has combined both sciences in half of a verse, when He states: "...Eat and drink but waste not by excess, for Allah loves not the wasters."'" (*Al-Qur'an*, 7:31)

The physician said: 'Why, then, has nothing been mentioned about medicine from the mouth of your Messenger?' Ibn Waquid replied: 'Our Messenger (saas), has combined the sciences about medicine in a few words when he says: "The stomach is the house for disease and prevention is the essence of medicine."' The Christian physician then said: 'Then your book, *Al-Qur'an*, and your Prophet Muhammad left nothing about medicine for Jalienas (a famous physician of the ancients).'" (Arkanul Arbaah)

An American physician published a report on fasting and its benefits saying: "It is mandatory on every person who is sick to restrain from food certain days in a year whether he be wealthy or poor because if bacteria can find food in abundance in the body, it will grow and multiply. But with fasting it becomes weak." He then praised Islam. It should be considered as the wisest religion, for as it mandated fasting it has mandated health care. He continued: "Indeed, Muhammad, who brought this religion, was the best physician who succeeded in his teachings, for he called for prevention before ailment, that is apparent in fasting and the nightly prayer (Taraweh) that Muslims observe after fast-breaking every day of Ramadan, for these physical acts contain big benefits in digesting food." (Siyaamuka Ayyuhal Muslim)

Patience

Fasting helps in conditioning the heart, the soul, and the body on the virtues of patience, tenacity, and firmness in the face of adversity. Patience is the pinnacle of self-mastery, discipline and spiritual agility. Patience is to turn the phrase "I can't" into

"I can." It is to say, the difficult is easy. It is an inner and psychological demolition of things perceived by others as impossible. Fasting helps in all these shades for the virtuous patient person because, the conditioning is that if a believer can exercise patience, and forsake gourmet food and drink, and the exhilaration we enjoy while eating or drinking our favorites, as well as marital association, and the gratifying of other normal appetites for a whole day, then for a month the realization that the barrier between you and food is your consciousness of your Creator, can better make you able to exercise patience in virtually everything in life.

Social Outlook

Socially, fasting is an expression of solidarity with the poor, the family and the whole society. This is a period in which the rich have first-hand experience of what it is to be poor, the pains the indigent suffers in normal living conditions. The process of disciplining resulting from Islamic fasting, instills in the rich the virtue of mercy, Rahmah, which is very important in terms of social well-being and proliferation of harmony. Allah bestows his mercy upon those who themselves are merciful to others. "Those who are merciful to others, the Merciful will have mercy upon them," the Messenger said. He continued, "Have mercy upon those on earth, and those in heaven will have mercy upon you." (Abu Dawud/Tirmidhi)

Family Ties

Fasting strengthens family ties, especially in that the family is an endangered institution in western society and throughout the world. It helps the family gather together to break fast, at *Iftar*, and eat *sahuur* together at least twice a day for a month. The family even makes Salaat, together with the father as Imam.

Fasting enhances and energizes friendship, as Ramadan is known as the month of invitations and visitations. Friends, family members and neighbors extend invitations to each other to come to their homes to have Iftar together. The Messenger said, "When a believer invites you, you should respond." Besides, Muslims gather together in the Masajid for *taraweh* and *ta'aleem*.

RAMADAN BELIEVERS

There are some Muslims who run away from all aspects of worship. They use all their energies, not for good deeds, but living a worldly life empty of faith. But come Ramadan, they will head home to Allah for repentance. They will become active again in prayer and fasting, and they will frequent the masajid. But no sooner are Ramadan and Eid over, then they return to their old habits, living on the edge again, putting on the garment of disbelief. These people should know Allah is not alive only in Ramadan. If they worship Allah only in Ramadan, it would be better for them just to stop worshipping altogether, because, as we mentioned earlier, if Ramadan does not benefit you the rest of the year, it is as if you did not have Ramadan at all.

COMPARISON BETWEEN THE FASTING IN ISLAM AND OTHER RELIGIONS

Al-Islam, has taken the lead in reforming the institution of fasting. This was a radical reform in the meaning, rules and purpose of the fast. It made the fast easy, natural and effective. The following are some of the points in this regard:

1. Fasting was a symbol of sadness, mourning, atonement for the sins, a reminder of disasters as well as self—mortification in Judaism and Christianity. Islam radicalized this doom and gloom concept of fasting, into an enlightened concept of triumph over the forces of evil. The month of fasting in Islam is a month of worship Muslims welcome each year with energy and happiness, and are saddened only when the month departs. This is contrary to the atmosphere of mourning. Fasting is for the living.

2. Fasting is not self-denial and punishment of the body and soul, a belief that was wide-spread among the medieval European ascetics. Indeed, there is not such a thing in Islam, nor in *Al-Qur'an* or the Sunnah. The laws that govern the institution are not extremely unbearable, the restrictions are not enforced 24 hours every day. The tradition of *sahuur* is a perfect example. The faster is allowed to delay and eat sahuur until he or she is certain that there are just a few minutes before morning prayer. Similarly, when it is time to break fast, the rule is to break as soon as the sun sets, with no delay. Besides, sleeping and resting during the day are all allowed. Working is not stopped and businesses are not closed down for the fast. In Judaism, working during the period

of fast is prohibited. Allah (SWT) said: "...Allah intends every facility for you. He does not want to put you to difficulties...." (Al-Qur'an, 2:185)

3. Fasting was for special classes of people in the previous religions. For the Brahmin class in the Hindu religion, fasting is mandatory only for the high priests. In some Latin religions, it is only women who must fast and there are no exceptions. (Arkanul Arba'ah)

4. In Judaism, the faster eats only after the break and there is no more food. The Arabs, before Islam, would not eat after sleeping. Islam, on the other hand, threw away all these human imposed restrictions. Allah said: "...And eat and drink, until the white thread of dawn appears to you distinct from it's black thread..." (Al-Qur'an, 2:187)

The person who makes a mistake in fasting is not punished, and the one who forgets and eats is forgiven.

5. Fasting in some other religions is based on a solar calendar, like the Gregorian calendar. This demands vast knowledge of calculation and astronomy in the making of a calendar. Besides, the months are fixed in a specific season, they do not rotate or change. Fasting in Islam is based on the lunar calendar and is tied to the sightings of *hilal*, the crescent, or new moon. Allah (SWT) states: "They ask you concerning the new moons. Say: They are but signs to mark fixed periods of time...." (Al-Qur'an, 2:189) And the hadith: "Eat until you see the crescent and break not until you see the crescent. If it is cloudy calculate the period of the month." (Muslim and others)

This enables Muslims in every corner of the earth, east and west, north and south, and all in between, in remote villages, on mountains, in conditions of illiteracy or literacy, in jungles or deserts, in inner cities to suburbs to start and end the fast all at the same time, without difficulty.

Why the moon instead of the sun as the basis for starting and ending fast? There are several reasons:

The lunar year is about ten or eleven days less compared to the Gregorian. Thus, if Ramadan 1990 began on March 27th, Ramadan in 1991 would begin around March 16th. Consequently, in the course of 36 years, every Muslim would have fasted every day of the year, the short days of the year, the long days of the year, the hot days and the cold days of the year. Muslims in different regions of the world would have had total equality in the number of days they fasted, and would have had an equal amount of seasonal and climatic changes. They would have an equal amount of cold or mild weather Ramadans.

If the fast were based on the Gregorian calendar, the Muslims in hot summer climates would have Ramadan during hot weather every year, forever. Some Muslims would have fasted long days while others short days, because Gregorian calendar months are fixed and immobile.

There is another interesting reason; fruits, vegetables for using the lunar calendar and some food items come in certain seasons. Fasting based on the lunar system means we may miss certain fruits in certain seasons, but by the end of the circle a Muslim would have tasted and tried different fruits during Ramadan, whereas fasting based on the Gregorian calendar would have prohibited some fruits during Ramadan, forever. This is why Muslims did not change the month of Ramadan, nor did they distort it by increasing or decreasing days, nor did they change it to different months.

FASTING IN CHRISTIANITY

The subject of fasting in Christianity is very difficult to discuss, simply because Christianity as a whole is very short on religious laws. Besides, there is fundamental disagreement among the scholars to whether Jesus (saas) commanded fasting. Fasting in Christianity seems to have evolved with time and is affected by social, political, and economic factors.

Jesus (saas) fasted 40 days before starting his mission. It is possible that he fasted on the Day of Atonement, which was an established tradition in Judaism. By the 4th century, there was no sign of 40 days of fasting in Christianity. There are traditions of fasting which differ greatly according to the country in which Christians live. The fast in Rome is different from the fast in Alexandria. Some abstain from meat, while others from fish and birds. Some will not eat fruits and eggs; some just fast on white bread. Some will abstain from all the above. Certain days had been made for fasting in later centuries to commemorate some events, such as the life of Jesus. There was a fast for three days in English law. During the time of Edward VI, James I, and the Elizabethan period, meat was prohibited during the fast, and King James I justified that by saying:

"The fishing industry and maritime commerce must become encouraged and it must be profitable." (Arkanul Arabaah)

This is why when Allah prescribed fasting, He says: "O you who believe! Fasting is prescribed to you as it was prescribed to those before you, that you may (learn) self restraint." *(Al-Qur'an, 2:184)*

BIDDING THE MONTH FAREWELL

Allah (SWT) has mandated on us three acts to observe at the end of Ramadan.

Zakatul-Fitr, Takbeer, and *'Eid Prayer.*

Takbeer

Allah has ordained upon the believers the utterance of *takbeer,* "Allah is the Greatest," at the conclusion of the month, Ramadan. Takbeer should start on the eve of 'Eid at sunset, and it continues until the time of 'Eid prayer. Allah (SWT) said: "...And complete the prescribed period and glorify Allah in that He has guided you and perchance you shall be grateful." *(Al-Qur'an, 2:185)*

The takbeer, Allah is the Greatest, is a superlative form indicating there is nothing in the creation that is bigger or greater than Allah. Everything in creation, things, ideas, institutions and planes, etc., pale into insignificance in the sight of Allah. This utterance is the believer's victory and national anthem upon the forces of evil, low desires, and our faith affirmation, song of obedience, and gratitude to Allah (SWT). Takbeer is always said when a Muslim reaches the summit, physical or spiritual, as in the completion of fast at the end of Ramadan. It takes greatness and remarkable inner strength to win one against the forces of evil, and the greatness goes to Allah.

The Formula for Takbeer

Allahu Akbar, Allahu Akbar
La illaha illa llah
Allahu Akbar Allahu Akbar
Wa lillahil hamd.

Allah is the Greatest, Allah is the Greatest. There is no deity worthy of worship but Allah, and Allah is greatest. Allah is the Greatest and all praise is due to Allah.

It is recommended for men to say the takbeer loud in the Masajid, homes, and market places as a sign of glorification of Allah, and expression of our gratitude and worship to Him. Women, however, should say it silently. Wouldn't it be excellent to see that the Muslim environment is charged with the glorification of Allah? Instead of neon lights, and outdoor decorations, and honking the horns of cars, Takbeer is our outward sign of the festivity.

The 'Eidul-Fitr is another important obligation after Ramadan and Sunnah of the Prophet. The details of this Eid can be found in the book *"The Prescribed Prayer Made Simple."*

THE BATTLE OF BADR

Ramadan is a source of spiritual as well as physical inspiration for Muslims. Physically, no month in our history has been more charitable and generous with victories than the month of Ramadan. One of the more remarkable examples is the Badr campaign (Battle of Badr). This was a battle in which the forces of truth, numbering 300 men, defeated an army three times their size against all odds. Badr is the name of a rural city about 150 miles from Madinah.

The day of the battle was named the Day of Criterion, *Yawmul Furqaan*, for Allah set apart the distinction between truth and falsehood by aiding His Messenger and the believers against all odds, and abandoning the unbelievers. All this took place in the month of Ramadan, in the second year of Hijrah. The reason for this encounter was purely coincidental. The Messenger of Allah (saas) was informed that his old antagonist and a political leader of the Quraysh, Abu Sufyan, was returning from Shaam (Northern Arabia) to Makkah with many camels in a large caravan.

The Messenger called upon his companions to intercept and confiscate the caravan which contained merchandise for Quraysh businessmen and women. The reason was because the Quraysh were in a state of war with the new ummah in Madinah, and because the Quraish had appropriated the wealth of the companions who were forced to flee Makkah because of their faith in Islam and suffer merciless persecution at the hand of Makkans. Furthermore, there was no treaty of nonbeligerance between the two parties.

Undoubtedly, the Muslims had every right to seize the contents of the caravan. Thus, the Messenger and the companions marched out of Madinah with 310 men with two horses and the 70 camels. Seventy of the men were *muhajireen* (immigrants from Makkah), and the rest were *ansaar* (the helpers from Madinah). Their objective was to capture the caravan. They did not intend to fight. But Allah, in His own will and wisdom determined otherwise, Allah (SWT) stated "That Allah might accomplish a matter already enacted" *(Al-Qur'an*, 8:44).

Abu Sufyan knew that he was being tailed so he dispatched a messenger to Makkah to inform them of the impending doom of their caravan, and urged them to swift action. Meanwhile, he drove the caravan off the desert's main highway and took a safer but longer coastal route instead, and escaped. The Quraysh, on the other hand, upon receiving this alarming news called for a general declaration of war.

The Quraysh were mighty and heavily prepared. Immediately, 1000 strong men were enlisted, including their warlords and generals. They amassed 100 horses and 700 camels. Their objective was to show off. Allah (SWT) stated: "And be not like those who started from their homes insolently and to be seen by men and to hinder (people) from the path of Allah..." *(Al-Qur'an*, 8:47) The army included singers to sing ill of the Muslims and dance at their defeat. When Abu Sufyan knew of their setting out, he sent them a message that the caravan had escaped, and that there was no need for the Quraysh to continue the journey, and urged them to return to Makkah and not to fight. The warmongers of the Quraysh refused to heed Abu Sufyan's call and insisted on continuing. The head of the pack, Abu Jahl (the Father of Ignorance), was reported as saying: "By Allah, we will not return until we reach Badr, spend three days there, slaughter camels, eat and drink wine and liquor, and let the Arabs hear about us so they will continue to fear us forever." (Ibn Hishaam)

As for the Messenger (saas), when he leaned that the Quraysh were heading towards Madinah, gathered his companions and sought their counsel in this grave matter. He told them, "Allah has promised me one of two groups, either the caravan or the army." Al-Miqdad bin Aswad (raa) stood up to represent the *muhajireen*, and said: "O Messenger of Allah, proceed with what Allah (SWT) commanded you. By Allah, we will not say to you what the Israelites said to their Prophet Musa: 'Go thou and thy lord and fight ye two while we sit here and watch.' Instead we will fight on your right, on your left, in your front and on your rear."

The head of Al-Aws, Sad bin Muaadh (raa), spoke on behalf of the ansaar, saying: "O Messenger of Allah, I hope you are not afraid that ansaar will not see it incumbent upon them to join you unless the enemy is in their homes. I would like to say on behalf of the ansaar: 'Go wherever you wish, connect the rope of whoever you wish, break the rope of whoever you wish, take from our wealth whatever you desire, give us out of it whatever you wish, whatever you take from us is better for us than what you leave, whatever you command of us we shall obey you. By Allah, if you decide to travel and take us with you until you reach the pool of Ghamdan, we will travel with you. If you ask us to cross a sea and you cross it we will cross it with you. We are not afraid to meet the enemy tomorrow. We are patient in war, truthful in the battlefield. Perhaps Allah will show you in us what will please your eyes.'"

The Messenger of Allah (saas) was delighted with what he heard from both the *muhajireen* and *ansaar* (raa). He said, "Go delightfully forward. By Allah, it is as if I am looking at the death places of the people."

The Messenger of Allah (saas) proceeded with the army of the Most Gracious until they camped at a well among the wells of Badr. When they were about to settle down, Al-Hubab bin Al-Mindhir Bin Amru bin Jamuh (raa) asked: "O Messenger of Allah, this place we settled in, is it a place Allah commanded us to camp in whereby we can not leave it? Or is it your idea of war strategy and tactics?" The Messenger replied, "It is my own idea of war strategy and tactics." He counselled "O Messenger of Allah, this is not a suitable place. Let us move to the well nearest to our enemy and settle down there while we cover up all the wells behind us with sand and palm trunks. We then should build on it a trough and fill it with our drinking water and they will not have any to drink." The Messenger liked the idea; he moved to the lower side with the city of Medinah at their back, and the Quraysh took the side that faced Makkah.

On the eve of the battle, Allah sent a mysterious rain. On the side of the Quraish it fell heavily. It soaked everything and created very slippery muddy conditions, making it difficult for the enemy's army to move forward. Whereas on the side of the Muslims, it was a light drizzle that refreshed them and cemented the sand and stabilized their movement.

The believers built a war booth on a hill overlooking the battlefield for their commander in chief, the Messenger of Allah (saas). He came down from the booth to straighten the lines of his companions and as he walked over the field he pinpointed the death spots of the enemy soldiers, he prophesied: "This is where so and so will fall, Allah willing; this is where so and so will fall." When the battle was over none of these people missed where they were supposed to fall and die, as the Messenger had pointed out before the war.

The Messenger then looked at his companions and at the Quraysh and said: "O Allah the Quraysh came with their vain glory, and boasting, and horses daring You, belying Your Messenger. O Allah, grant me Your assistance that You promised me. O Allah, accomplish for me that which You promised me. O Allah, I remind You of Your promise and Your decree. O Allah, if You willed You would never be worshipped. O Allah, If this army is defeated today You will never be worshipped." (Ibn Hishaam)

Muslims sought help from Allah and He answered them, as He stated: "Remember thy Lord inspired the angels (with the message): I am with you, give firmness to the believers I will instil terror into the hearts of the unbelievers, smite ye all their fingerstips off them. This because they contended against Allah and His Apostle. If any contend against Allah and His apostle, Allah is strict in punishment." (Al-Qur'an, 8:12–13)

The two armies met in a fierce battle. The fighting intensified and went on and on. The Messenger was in his war camp and with him was Abubakr and Saad bin Muaadh guarding him. The Messenger in the meantime, was praying to Allah for help and victory. He napped for a little while and woke up to encourage the Muslims and to promise: "Nay, the hour of Judgement is the time promised them, for their Hour will be Most grievous and most bitter." (Al-Qur'an, 54:46) He encouraged his companions to fight, and said: "I swear by the One in whose hand Muhammad's soul is, any man who fights them today and is killed while he is patient in the ordeal and seeks the pleasure of Allah, going forward and not backing off, Allah will enter him into Paradise." (Ibn Hishaam)

Umair bin Himaam Al-Ansaari (raa) stood up with a few dates in his hand and was about to eat them, and asked: "O Messenger of Allah, a paradise whose width is like the width of heavens and earth?" the Messenger responded: "Yes." Umair said: "Bakhin! Bakhin! (indicating strong appreciation and acceptance) O Messenger of Allah, there is nothing between me and paradise except to be killed by these people. If I live to eat these dates that will be a long life. Then he threw the dates away and fought until he was killed.

The Messenger (saas) took a handful of sand or stones and threw them at the enemy soldiers and no one was hit by this sand but it blinded and preoccupied them. This was a divine intervention from Allah. The enemy soldiers could not fight after that and they were defeated. The remaining soldiers flew from the battlefield in all directions and the Muslims went after them. Seventy of them were killed and seventy were taken as prisoners of war.

Twenty four of the dead were the warlords of the Quraysh whom, the Messenger ordered to be thrown into a well. They included the arch-infidel, Abu Jahl, Ahaibah bin Rabeeah and his brother Utbah and his son Al-Waleed bin Utbah. Abdullah bin Masud (raa) reported that the Messenger (saas) faced the Kaabah and prayed over these four and said: "I bear witness that I saw them dead. The sun has changed their appearance because it was a hot day." (Ibn Hishaam)

After the war the Messenger (saas) stayed at Badr for three days, and as he was riding his horse, on the third day, he pulled away where he came to the edge of a well. He stood and started to call the dead among the enemies by their full names and the names of their fathers. "O so and so, the son of such and such, are you happy that you have disobeyed Allah and His Messenger, for we found what Allah promised us in truth have you found what Allah promised you in truth?" Umar (raa) and many companions, inquired in astonishment "O Messenger of Allah, why do you speak to bodies that have no souls?" The Messenger replied: "I swear by the One in whose hand Muhammad's soul is, you do not hear what I say more than they do."

As for the prisoners of war, the Messenger asked his companions their opinions. Saad bin Muaadh (raa) commented: "This is the first defeat for the polytheists. I would have preferred the continuation of the battle than to have taken men as prisoners of war." Umar bin Khattab (raa) said: "I think that it would have been better to allow us to kill them. Allow Ali bin Abi Talib to kill Aqeel and allow me a member of my family, for these people are the leaders of the unbelief." Abu Bakr, on the other hand, said: "These are our uncles and families. I think it would be better to take ransom from them to strengthen ourselves with funds, perhaps Allah will guide them into Islam." The Messenger took ransom from them. Most of them gave between four to a 100 *dirham*. Some provided services by teaching the Muslim children of Madinah the basics of reading and writing, others by freeing a

Muslim bonds man or woman in Makkah. Some were killed because of their crimes against Muslims, while others were let go.

The lessons of this battle are very obvious. An army outnumbered three to one was victorious because it was fighting in the path of Allah, because it stood firm to raise the banner of Allah and to defend Allah's religion, so Allah helped them. Anyone who stood on the same principle, the result would be the same. Indeed, Ramadan is not a period to slacken, it is a serious time in which serious decisions are taken and higher goals are achieved.

CONQUEST OF MAKKAH

As in the Battle of Badr, the month of Ramadan was the time in which Allah chose to grant the believers their biggest victory ever. In the eighth year of Hijrah in the Islamic calendar, Allah (SWT) delivered the sacred city of Makkah to the Muslims, virtually without any resistance or bloodshed. With this victory Allah rescued this great city from the yoke of *shirk* (polytheism); it became an Islamic city forever, the city in which *tawheed* replaced *shirk* and belief replaced disbelief, and Islam and submission to Allah unseated obstinacy and haughtiness. The worship of Allah was finally declared and the idols were smashed. During the 6th year of Hijrah, the Messenger of Allah and the Quraysh signed the famous treaty of Hudaybiyah, which included the clause that any tribe that desired to join either party, the Quraysh or Muslims might do so. The Khuzaah tribesmen decided to join the Messenger of Allah, and Banu Bakar decided to join the Quraysh.

There was bad blood between the two tribes, a pre-Islamic blood grudge. Banu Bakar seized on this opportunity and attacked the Khuzaah without any provocation, while Quraysh, in violation of the treaty, secretly gave their allies all the help they asked for, men and supplies.

Khuzaah had no choice but to inform the Messenger, their ally, that Banu Bakar and their allies Quraysh had unilaterally broken the treaty of Hudaybiyah by attacking them. The Messenger promised them, "I will prevent from you what I will prevent from myself." (Ibn Hishaam)

The Quraish realized they had broken the treaty with the Messenger by attacking the Muslims' allies. Realizing the gravity of the situation, they dispatched Abu Sufyan to Madinah on a mission of fence-mending and to beg for mercy and apologize for their misdeed. Upon his arrival, Abu Sufyan went to his daughter

Umm Habeebah (raa), the Prophets's wife, and when he wanted to sit on the Messenger's carpet she folded it up so that he could not sit on it. "My dear daughter," he asked, "I hardly know if you think that the carpet is too good for me or that I am too good for the carpet!" She responded, "This is the Messenger's carpet and you are a dirty polytheist. I do not want you to sit on the Messenger's carpet." Abu Sufyan knew then that this mission was impossible. He then went to meet the Messenger to apologize, review and extend the treaty. He spoke to the Messenger (saas) but he was disappointed because he got no response.

His request was met with total rejection as he attempted to enlist the help of Abubakr, Umar and Ali respectively. As the gates closed in his face, he returned to Ali for advice. Ali said he knew no measure that would correct the explosive situation.

Finally, Abu Sufyan returned to Makkah totally disheartened because he knew the future was bleak. When he arrived in Makkah, the Quraysh gathered around to find out the result of his mission. "Totally unsuccessful," he told them. He narrated how his efforts with the Messenger, Abubakr and Umar and Ali were met with total rejection.

Ali was the most polite of all. Therefore, he again went to Ali before he headed home and asked for advice. Ali told him since he was the chief of Banu Kinanah, he could invoke on behalf of his tribe willingness to make peace with Muhammad. Abu Sufyan asked Ali whether that would be of any use, and Ali replied that he was not sure, but he could have nothing to tell him until after the Messenger had decided what to do. Abu Sufyan's listeners asked whether the idea to go in front of the people was approved by Muhammad, and he replied no. They told him Ali had played with his mind.

The Messenger, on the other hand, had called his companions to prepare for war. Unlike other battles, where he concealed his destination, this time he told them exactly where they would be heading. Prophet Muhammad (saas) asked the tribes around the Islamic state to enlist in the battle. He demanded that the battle plans be kept secret from the enemy until they reached Makkah because he wanted to surprise them.

While the Messenger and the believers were preparing for the campaign, an insidious incident was taking place. It was reported that Hatib Abu Balta'a betrayed the Messenger by writing a letter to Quraysh, telling them that the Messenger intended to invade them. He gave the letter to a woman to deliver and paid her for her services. She put the letter on her head and then plaited her hair over it and started off. The Messenger, through revelation, was informed of Hatib's action, and he sent Ali *(karamallahu wajhahu)* and Az-Zubair bin Al-Awwam (Radiyallahu'anhu) with instructions to go after her.

When they overtook her they dismounted and searched her bags but found nothing. Ali swore by Allah that the Messenger could not be mistaken nor could they, and warned the lady that if she did not produce the letter they would strip her. When she realized that he was earnest, she told him to turn aside, and then she let down her braids and drew out the letter, and gave it to him and he took it to the Messenger of Allah.

The Messenger summoned Hatib and asked him what induced him to act the way he did. He replied that he believed in Allah and his Messenger and had never ceased to do so, but that he was not a man of standing among the Quraysh and that he had a son and family there and that he had to deal prudently with them for their sakes. Umar (raa) wanted to cut off his head for his hypocritical act, but the Messenger asked him "How do you know, Umar? Perhaps Allah looked favorably on those who were at Badr," And said: "Do as you please, for I have forgiven you."

Upon this serious incident Allah revealed: "O ye who believe, take not My enemies and yours as friends (or protectors), offering them your love even though they have..." (Al-Qur'an, 60:1-4) Meanwhile, the Messenger (saas) marched out of Madinah with about 10,000 men, leaving Abdullah bin Umm Maktum (raa) in charge of Madinah. When he reached Juhfah, he met his uncle Al-Abbas with his entire family, migrating to Medinah to embrace Islam. At Al-Abwaa he met his uncles Abu Sufyan and Abdullah bin Abi Umayyah, both of whom were passionate enemies of Islam and the Messenger. They announced their belief in Islam, and it was accepted from them. About Abu Sufyan, the Messenger said: "I hope he will succeed Hamzah," who had been killed during the Battle of Uhud.

The news of the Muslims' movement was so tightly controlled that no Makkan knew of their approach until they were close to Makkah. The Messenger of Allah stopped there and ordered the army to set 10,000 bonfires. Umar was guarding the Messenger. Because his movement was so unknown, he needed to tell the Quraysh himself that he was at their door-steps. Thus, he sent Al Abbas to inform any person he could find about the Muslims' arrival, so that they could come to him and seek some kind of peaceful resolution in order to prevent any bloodshed in the Sacred City.

While Al-Abbas was on his lookout, he heard Abu Sufyan saying to his comrade, Badeel bin Zurqaa: "I have never seen a fire this big in my life." Badeel replied this might be the Khuzaah army. Abu Sufyan said the Khuzaah was smaller than this. Al-Abbas recognized his voice and called to him. Abu Sufyan answered and asked, "What do you want, Abal Fadl?" Al-Abbas replied, "I am the messenger of the Messenger of Allah and his army of believers is heading this way." Abu Sufyan, shocked and terrified, asked, "What should I do?" Al-Abbas said, "Ride with me to the Messenger and I will protect you."

When Abu-Sufyan was in front of him, the Messenger (saas) demanded: "Woe to you Abu Sufyan. Is it not time for you to know that there is no deity but Allah." He replied: "By my father and mother, you know that if there were any deity beside Allah it would have helped me. The Messenger continued: "Is it not time for you to know that I am the Messenger of Allah." Abu Sufyan hesitated for a while, so Al-Abbas encouraged him: "Woe to you. Announce your Islam." Abu Sufyan then declared the *Shahadah*, the declaration of faith.

The Messenger told Al-Abbas to take Abu Sufyan to the foot of the valley and let him see the Muslim soldiers marching. The army paraded past Abu Sufyan, squadron after squadron. No squadron would pass but Abu Sufyan asked, "Who are those?" While they were watching, a squadron commanded by Saad bin Ubadah (raa) passed. When they were passing, Abu Sufyan overheard Saad saying: "Today is the day of battle, the day of great war, the day when all taboos will be lifted."

Hearing this, Abu Sufyan was alarmed, so when the Messenger passed by him Abu Sufyan told him what Saad had just said. The Messenger said: "Saad lied to you. This is the day in which the Kaabah will be glorified, the day in which the Kaabah will be adorned." Then the Messenger commanded that Saad be relieved of his duty as commander and that his post be given to his son Qais, so he would not be too much offended because it would remain in his family. Had Saad been permitted to proceed, this would have violated the Messenger's commandment that no blood should be shed in Makkah.

The Messenger proceeded to Makkah, commanding his flags to be concentrated in the area of Al-Hujun. He entered Makkah, a victorious conqueror bowing down his head as a sign of humbleness to Allah (SWT). He bowed until his head could be seen touching his horses neck. Meanwhile, he was reciting: "Verily We have granted thee a manifest victory." (Al-Qur'an, 48:1) He repeated it several times.

He put Khalid bin Waleed and Az-Zubair bin Awwam on each side of the Muslim army. The Messenger declared: "Whoever enters into the Masjid he is safe, whoever enters into the house of Abu Sufyan he is safe, whoever enters his own house and closes the door he is safe." The Messenger entered the Masjid Al-Haram and made circumambulation on his horse. There were about 360 idols around the Kaabah. He pulled them down with his sword while reciting: "And say: 'Truth has arrived and falsehood has perished for falsehood is by its nature bound to perish.'" (Al-Qur'an, 17:81) Also "Say: Truth has arrived and falsehood neither creates anything new nor restores anything.'" (Al-Qur'an, 34:49) The idols tumbled on their faces.

The Messenger entered the Kaabah and ordered all the pictures to be destroyed. He prayed inside, and afterward he walked round saying *Allahu Akbar* (Allah is the Greatest), in every corner declaring the oneness of Allah (SWT). When he came out of the Kaabah, he stood in the door and said: "There is no deity but Allah alone; He has no associates. He has made good His promise and helped His servant. He has put to flight the confederates. Every claim of privilege, of blood or property is abolished by me except the custody of the House of Allah and water for the pilgrims. The unintentional slaying in a quasi-intentional way by club or whip, for him the blood wit is most severe: a hundred camels, forty of them to be pregnant. O Quraysh, Allah has taken from you the haughtiness of paganism and its veneration of ancestors. Man springs from Adam and Adam springs from dust." Then he recited to them this verse. "O Mankind, We created you from male and female and made you into peoples and tribes that you may know one another: of a truth the most noblest of you in Allah's sight is the most pious." (Al-Qur'an, 49:13)

He continued: "'O Quraysh, what do you think that I am about to do with you?' They replied 'Good. You are a noble son of a noble brother.' 'Well, I would say to you what Prophet Yusuf said to his brothers: "This day let no reproach be cast on you: Allah will forgive you and He is the most Merciful of those who show mercy."'" (Al-Qur'an, 12:92) He said: "Go your way for you are freed ones." (Ibn Hishaam)

On the second day of the campaign the Messenger (saas) addressed all of Makkah. He said: "Allah made Makkah holy the day He created heavens and earth, and it will be holy until the Day of Resurrection. It is not lawful for anyone who believes in Allah and the last day to shed blood therein, nor to cut down trees therein. It was not lawful to any one before me and it will not be lawful to anyone after me. Indeed, it is not lawful for me except at this time because of Allah's anger against its people. Now it has regained its former holiness. Let those here now tell those that are not here. If anyone should say, the Messenger killed men in Makkah, say Allah permitted His Messenger to do so but he does not permit you." The hour that Allah permitted the Messenger was from sunrise to late afternoon on the day of campaign.

The Messenger stayed in Makkah 29 days, while shortening his prayers. He stayed to educate the newly converted Makkans in the basic teachings of Islam, *tawheed*, to reinforce their *iman*, and take allegiance from the people. In Bukhari, Mujashie (raa) said: "I brought my brother to the Messenger of Allah (saas) to give *bayah* (allegiance) to the Messenger on Hijrah (migration). The Messenger replied: "The people of Hijrah have taken the reward of Hijrah, but I will accept your allegiance on Islam, *iman* and *jihad*." With this great victory, people entered into the fold of Islam in droves *(jama'at)*."

THE ELEMENTS OF VICTORY

Allah (SWT) granted the believers victory after victory in different campaigns, in Badr, Makkah, Hunayn, Quds, in Spain, and many other places. Allah's help to the believers, is the fulfillment of His promise. He never reneges on His words. "...And it was due from Us to aid those who believe." (Al-Qur'an, 30:47) He helped them because they sought to establish His religion that He proclaimed over all other religions. Whoever holds to it, He will grant them victory. He helped them because they held to the spiritual and material cause of victory. They had the will and discipline that superseded that of their enemies. They acted according to the plan that Allah charted for them, as He said: "So lose no heart nor fall into despair; for ye must gain mastery if ye are true in faith. If a wound has touched you, be sure a similar wound has touched the others. Such days (of varying fortunes) We give to men and men by turns, that Allah may know those that believe, and that He may take to Himself from your ranks martyr-witnesses to truth. And Allah loves not those that do wrong." (Al-Qur'an, 3:139–140)

With these directives, the Muslims acted with strength, determination and seriousness. They prepared and subscribed to all elements of power, physical and otherwise, as Allah (SWT) states: "Against them make ready your strength to the utmost of your power..." (Al-Qur'an, 8:60) With this strength Allah aided them because they aided His cause and His religion of Islam. "...Allah will certainly aid those who aid His cause, for verily Allah is full of strength, exalted in Might (able to enforce His will). Also they are those who if We establish them in the land, establish regular prayer and give regular charity, enjoin the right and forbid wrong. With Allah rests the end (and decision) of (all) affairs." (Al-Qur'an, 22:40–41)

In this verse are the attributes that lead to this victory:

First, for us to be established on the earth as *khulafah*, rulers we must observe total *ubudiyah* (worship) of Allah alone. If we obey and worship Allah sincerely in our hearts, pronouncements, deeds, and will, and if we do not intend with that action anything but the pleasure of Allah and the last day, and if we do not desire position, praise from people and our peers, wealth, or anything from this world, and this *ebadah* continues in all aspects of our life, only then will Allah (SWT), if he so wills, grant us, to use the Quranic term, *tamkeen* (establish in authority and *khilafah*).

Allah states: "Allah has promised to those among you who believe and work righteous deeds, that he will of a surety grant them in the land, inheritance (of power), as He granted it to those before them; that He will establish in authority their religion, the one which He has chosen for them; and that He will change (their state) after the fear in which they (lived), to one of security and peace. They will worship Me (alone) and not associate aught with Me. If any do reject faith after this, they are rebellious and wicked." *(Al-Qur'an, 24:55)*

Second, by establishing Salaat: that is, to observe it in the way the Messenger observed it. Be mindful of its prerequisites, pillars, obligations, rules, and regulations. Cleanliness must be perfected, standing, bowing, prostration, and sitting must all be observed properly. Be heedful of the time of each and every prayer, *Jumah* and *jamaah* prayers. Observe Salaat with humility and complete Allah-consciousness, which is the spirit of the body of Salaat. Without it there is no Salaat. In a hadith related by

Ammar bin Yasir (raa), he said: "I heard the Messenger of Allah say "Verily, a man may turn away from Salaat and nothing is written for him of that Salaat but the tenth or ninth, eighth, seventh, sixth, fifth, fourth, third or half." (Abu Dawud)

Third, is by Zakaat: that is, to give Zakaat to its lawful and rightful recipients willingly and without any rancor or ill feeling, to give a complete amount without cheating, so as to seek the pleasure of Allah (SWT).

Fourth, by enjoining what is right, *(amru bil maaruf)*. This means upholding or helping others to uphold anything that Allah (SWT) and His Messenger commanded or instructed of us. One of the main objectives of enjoining what is right is to revive and maintain the *shareeah* of Allah on the earth. To be actively involved in reforming the believers and servants of Allah, so as they will stay the cause of straight path, *siraatul mustaqeem*, and to intend with this, Allah's mercy and His pleasure.

Fifth, by forbiding what is wrong, *nahyu anil munkar.* This means personally avoiding or helping others avoid everything that Allah (SWT) or His Messenger forbade, the big or small sins, things that relate to acts of worship, behavior and conduct and relationship with the believers. This aspect protects the religion and the people, and prevents fasad (evil acts) from seeping into the body of the *ummah.*

Enjoining what is right and forbidding what is wrong are the two most important pillars of Islam. They are necessary for the survival of the ummah, its power, and its unity, so that the ummah would not be weakened by peoples' desires and end up going in different directions. This is why these two principles (enjoining the good and forbidding the wrong) are among the obligatory duties of a believer if he or she is able. Allah (SWT) commands:

"Let there arise out of you a band of people inviting to all that is good, enjoining what is right and forbidding what is wrong. They are the ones to attain felicity. Be not like those who are divided amongst themselves and fall into disputations after receiving clear signs. For them is a dreadful penalty." (Al-Qur'an, 3:104–105)

Were it not for this principle, the ummah would have been dissolved, as is our situation today. Allah declares: "You are the best of people, evolved for mankind, enjoining what is right, forbidding what is wrong and believing in Allah..." (Al-Qur'an, 3:110) By neglecting this principle, Allah cursed the Israelites, as He states: "Curses were pronounced on those among the children of Israel who rejected faith, by the tongue of Dawuud, and of Jesus *(Isa)* the son of Mary, because they disobeyed and persisted in excesses. Nor did they (usually) forbid one another the iniquities which they committed: evil indeed were the deeds which they did." (Al-Qur'an, 5:81)

Whenever these five elements are fulfilled, along with what Allah exhorted us to, victory will come, provided we cultivate determination, perseverance, and prepare for physical strength. This is what we are promised, and Allah will never renege or break His promise. Allah states: "(It is) the promise of Allah. Never does Allah depart from His promise; but most men understand not. They know but the outer (things) in the life of this world: but of the end of things they are heedless." (Al-Qur'an, 30:6–7) Only then will victory be accomplished in a way that no one thought possible.

The believer who has total trust in Allah's promise is aware that physical elements — as vital as they are — no matter how strong, are not enough and are nothing compared to the power of Allah Who created this strength. The people of Aad boasted of their power. "Who is more powerful than us?" they said. Allah responded, saying: "...Did they not see that Allah, Who created them, was superior to them in strength. But they continued to reject Our Signs! So We sent against them a furious wind through days of disaster, that We might give them a taste of the penalty of humiliation in this life; but the penalty of a Hereafter will be more humiliating still, and they will find no help." (Al-Qur'an, 41:15–16)

Pharaoh was proud of his vast domain and the rivers that flowed beneath it, so Allah (SWT) drowned him in the same water he was proud of. Further, Allah made Prophet Musa (ass) inherit his kingdom and his people, whereas he was perceived by Pharaoh as weak and unable to express himself. The Quraysh were intoxicated by their power and vainglory. They left their homes in a campaign to demonstrate their power and to terrorize the entire Arabian region. They were advised to return home, but refused, and continued to march to Badr for an engagement with destiny. So Allah made them pay a heavy price and taste the most humiliating defeat; the defeat that let them become the laughing — stock of all of Arabia and the world over from that day on.

If we today, in this day in time, take heed of the numerous warnings of Allah, and establish our religion and become leaders of this erring world, not following or imitating others, and take all the physical means of modern times and spiritual means from our Book with sincerity, Allah will help us as He helped our ancestors. Allah made good His promise and helped His servants, and He put to fight the confederate alone. "(Such has been) the practice (approved) of Allah already in the past: no change wilt thou find in the practice (approved) of by Allah." (Al-Qur'an, 48:23).

RETREAT *(AL-I'ETIKAAF)*

I'etikaaf is from the root word *"Akafa"* to adhere, cling, stick or keep. It means to engage and to devote something, to a thing, be it good or bad. Allah (SWT) states in Al-Qu'ran:

"...What are these images to which ye are (so assiduously) devoted?" (Al-Qu'ran 21:52)

In *Shari'ah* it means to engage in a retreat in the Masjid and stay there with the intention of seeking nearness to Allah the Almighty, and His reward.

Its Legalization

The majority of Muslim scholars agree that *I'etikaaf* is permissible, for the Messenger of Allah (saas) observed *I'etikaaf* in the Month of Ramadan during the last ten days. In his last Ramadan he observed it 20 days, as is related by Bukhari and others. Besides, his companions and wives observed it during his lifetime and after.

I'etikaaf can be either Sunnah or obligatory, *wajib*. The Sunnah *I'etikaaf* is when a Muslim volunteers to seek nearness to Allah, and to imitate the Messenger by observing this kind of *'ebadah*, and the Sunnah is meritorious in the last ten days of Ramadan.

The obligatory *I'etikaaf* is the one when a believer makes it obligatory on himself, by invoking a conditional vow, such as saying: I am vowing in the Name of Allah to engage in retreat; or if Allah cures my sick relative, I will engage in *I'etikaaf*. In Bukhari, the Messenger of Allah (saas) said: "Whoever vowed to obey Allah, should obey him." In the same hadith, Umar (ra) told the Messenger (saas), "I vowed to engage in a night retreat in the Sacred Masjid," and the Messenger responded, "Fulfil your vow." (Bukhari)

Time Of Retreat

The mandatory retreat can be observed according to the vow of the vower. If he vowed to retreat a day or more, it becomes necessary for him to fulfil it. But voluntary retreat has no time limit. It may be done by staying in the masjid with the intention of *I'etikaaf* for short or long periods of time, and the person will be rewarded so far as he remains in the masjid. If he leaves the masjid and returns, he should restate his *niyah* (intention).

The one who is in retreat may cut off his *I'etikaaf*, when he feels like it, before the time that he had intended. 'Aishah (ra), the Messenger's wife, said: "Whenever the Messenger intends to engage in retreat he will pray his *Fajr*, then he begins his *I'etikaaf*." She continued, "One day the Messenger intended to engage in retreat the last ten days of Ramadan, and he ordered his tent to be built. When I saw that, I asked for my own tent to be built, and the rest of his wives asked for the same thing. After *Fajr* prayer, he looked at the tents, what do you intend with this righteousness?' So he asked his tent and his wives to be removed, then he delayed his *I'etikaaf* to the first ten days of Shawwal." (Bukhari) This report is an indication that it is permissible to disengage from the retreat after starting.

The Prerequisites of Retreat

For a retreat to be valid, the observer must be Muslim, must have reached puberty, and must be pure from *janabah*, (major defilement, menstruation, and post-childbirth bleeding). People who are impure cannot engage in *I'etikaaf*.

The Pillars of Al-I'etikaaf

There are two pillars for *I'etikaaf*: intention, and staying in the Masjid. Niyyah or intention has been discussed earlier, but regarding staying in the masjid, Allah states:

"...But do not associate with your wives while you are in retreat in the masajid..." (*Al-Qu'ran 2:187*) This verse prohibits two things: marital relationships during *I'etikaf* because this contradicts the spirit of devotion, and observing *I'etikaf* in any place but a masjid. Thus, any believing man or woman who desires to observe *I'etikaaf* may do so only in a masjid as we see the Messenger's wives were building their tents in the masjid.

Masjid In Which *I'etiqaaf* Can Be Held.

Some scholars are of the opinion that any masjid in which the five daily prayers are observed can be used for retreat, but this opinion is based on a weak hadith. Imams Malik and Shafie and others said *I'etikaaf* is permissible in any masjid because the verse is general, and did not single out or specify any particular masjid.

The retreater can not leave the masjid, but he can leave his tent to join the congregational prayer, and clime the minaret for *adhan*. But, if he steps out of the masjid the retreat is invalid.

The majority of scholars said if the masjid is in a house — such as a room in a house turned into a masjid, it cannot be used as a place for *I'etikaaf* because it does not have the name "masjid," and it may be sold; whereas, you can not sell a masjid, (unless it is to be sold in order to build a new one on the same spot, or move it somewhere else).

Vowing *I'etiqaaf* in a Special Masjid

Whoever vowes to engage in *I'etikaaf* in the Masjid Al-Haran, the Messenger's Masjid, or Masjid Al-Aqsa, he should make it in the masjid that he intended. But if he vowes to engage in retreat in any masjid, he can I'etikaaf in any masjid anywhere because no masjid, (except the three mentioned above), is better than another masjid.

If he vowed to engage in retreat in Masjid An-Nabawi he can do it in Masjid Al-Haram, because the latter is better in merit than the former.

Fasting In Retreat

If the retreater fasts, it is good, if not the retreat is still valid. In a hadith reported earlier 'Umar told the Messenger that he had vowed to observe retreat one night during the pre-Islamic *(Jahiliyah)* period in the *Masjid Al-Haraam*. The Messenger responded "Fulfil your vow." In the hadith, there is an indication that fasting is not necessary for *I'etikaaf* because Umar (ra) vowed *I'etikaaf* at night and the Prophet told him to fulfil his vow and there is no fasting at night.

The Beginning and Ending Time Of *I'etikaaf*

There is no specific time for beginning or ending *I'etikaaf*. Whenever one enters into the masjid with *niyyah*, he begins his retreat. If he intends to engage in I'etikaaf the last ten days of Ramadan, he should prepare his tent before sunset. In a hadith related by Abu Saed, the Messenger of Allah said: "Whoever intends to retreat with me should retreat during the last ten nights (of Ramadan)." (Al-Bukhari). The first night of the ten is the night of the 21st of Ramadan because in Islam the days begin at sunset. However, the reports that said the Messenger (saas) entered his I'etikaaf place after Fajr prayer do not mean he started after Fajr, they mean he returned to his place of I'etikaaf at that time.

If I'etikaaf is for the last ten days of Ramadan, the observer should leave after sunset the last day of the month, but it is preferred that he remains in the masjid and should not leave it until the time of Eid. If a person intends to engage in I'etikaaf for a day, or several days, as voluntary I'etikaaf, he will enter into his place of I'etikaaf before the break of dawn and will leave after sunset, whether it is in Ramadan or not. If a person intends to engage in I'etikaaf for a night or two as a voluntary act, he should enter before sunset and leave after the break of dawn.

The reason is the night begins with the sunset and completes with the break of dawn, and the day begins with the break of dawn and completes with sunset. If a believer intends to engage in I'etikaaf for a month he should enter the first night of the month before sunset and leave after sunset when the month finishes.

What a Retreater Should Engage In

It is recommended that the retreater should engage in supererogatory worship, prayer, recitation of Al-Qu'ran, Glorification of Allah, Praising Allah, frequent declaration of Kalimat, Takbeer, seeking forgiveness from Allah, invoking Allah's blessing on the Messenger of Allah, and supplications, as well as any act of worship that will bring the servant nearer to Allah. Included in these acts of worship is studying the books of Tafseer, hadith, the life history of the Prophets, as well as any books on fiqh and religion. He should build a retreat (store his provisions) in the corner of the masjid where he or she will not disturb the regular worshippers.

He should not concern himself with what does not concern him, which is the best way to seek nearness to Allah. In a hadith reported by Ibn 'Abbass (raa), the Messenger of Allah (saas), was delivering a sermon, khutbah, and a man stood up but would not talk. A companion said, "This is Abu Israeal. He vowed to not stand, nor sit, nor seek shade, nor speak, but fast." The Messenger (saas) said, "Command him to speak and seek shade, to sit and complete his fast." (Bukhari, Ibn Ma Jaa and Abu Dawuud). In a related report the Messenger of Allah (saas) stated: "No person can be called orphan after puberty; and no person should remain silent all day and night." (Abu Dawuud)

What Is Permitted Of Retreater

He may leave the retreat and go out to bid farewell to his family. Safiyah (raa) said: "The Messenger of Allah (sas) was in his retreat, so I came to visit him at night. I spoke to him, and when I was leaving he stood to bid me farewell. On their way two men of Ansaur saw the Messenger (saas) and started to run fast. The Messenger told them: slowly, you don't need to run, she is Safiyah bint Huyayy, (my wife; don't think I am walking with another sister)' they said in surprise: 'Glory be to Allah, O Messenger of Allah!' (for they were baffled for what he said to them.) 'The Messenger said The Satan circulates in the human system the same way the blood circulates, so I was afraid that Satan might throw or whisper (ill thoughts) in your heart.'" (Bukhari/ Muslim) The Prophet, (saas) left his retreat. Thus it is permissible to leave.

It is permitted to comb one's hair, shave, trim the nails, clean the body, wear one's best clothes and use perfume. In a report by 'Aishah (raa), she said: "The Messenger used to be in *I'etikaaf* and he would put his head through the window and I would wash it for him, while I was in my menstruation." (Muslim/Bukhari)

It is permitted for him to leave the masjid to take care of essential things. The scholars agreed that the retreater is permitted to leave to eat and drink and to use the toilet, also to leave the masjid to purify the body from *janabah* and to clean the clothes.

It is permitted to eat and drink and sleep in the masjid, but extreme care should be taken to safeguard the cleanliness of the Masjid. The person may be a party to weddings and some legal contracts taking place in the masjid during the *I'etikaaf*.

Things That Invalidated *Al-I'etikaaf*

Exiting from the masjid without any good reason, even if it is for a moment, because that is one of its pillars.

Apostasy *(riddah)* for it contradicts *ebadah*. Allah (SWT), states:

"But it has already been revealed to thee as it was to those before thee, if thou were to join gods with Allah, truly fruitless will be thy work (in life) and thou will surely be in the ranks of those who lose (all spiritual good)." (Al-Qur'an, 39:65)

Insanity due to madness, drugs or intoxicants, for sanity is prerequisite in all forms of worship.

Menstruation (hayd) and post-childbirth bleeding (nifaas).

Martial relations. Allah states:

"...But do not associate with wives while you are in retreat in the masaajid." *(Al-Qur'an, 2:187)*

Nothing is wrong with touching one's spouse provided it is free from passion. This does not include kissing. If one kisses or touches his spouse with passion, he or she has done wrong, for it contradicts the spirit of *I'etikaaf*, but the *I'etikaaf* is valid provided he does not discharge semen. That is according to Imams Abu Hanifah and Ahmed. Imam Malik, on the other hand, said in this instance, the *I'etikaaf* becomes invalid because this is illegal association, even without discharge of semen. The reason for the difference of opinion is the interpretation of the word *"association"* *(mubasharah)*.

Originally *baashara* means to touch, scrape off; or to have sexual intercourse. The point here is an *usuulul Fiqh*, Islamic legal theory question. That is, does the word that implies both actual and metaphorical have a general implication, *aam*, or not? Those who say it has a general implication, *aam*, say *mubasharah* in the above verse means actual marital intercourse and any association that is less than intercourse. Those who say it does not have a general implication say *mubasharah* here means only sexual relations. *Allahu 'Alam* (Allah is the best knower).

Redemption of *I'etikaaf*

Whoever starts *I'etikaaf* voluntarily and then breaks, it is recommended to redeem it. But if he vows a day, or two, then starts and then invalidates it, he must redeem it whenever he is able, according to the majority of the scholars. If he died before making it up, redemption is not necessary, however, Imam Ahmed said: "His next of kin should redeem it for him."

ZAKAAT *(ALMS)*

Ramadan is the month of giving and benevolence, the Messenger was more benevolent than a falling rain. Muslims are encouraged to emulate the Messenger of Allah (saas), to assess and pay their Zakaat during the month of Ramadan, thus combining the two pillars of Islam at the same time.

Zakaat (alms) is the name of what a believer returns out of his or her wealth to the neediest of Muslims for the sake of the Almighty Allah. It is called Zakaat because the word Zakaat is from Zakaa which means, to increase, purify and bless.

Who Should Give Zakaat

The obligation of Zakaat is mandatory on every Muslim who possesses the minimum Nisaab, whether the person is man, woman, young, old sane or insane. Because the proof of Zakaat in Al-Qur'an and Sunnah is general and does not exclude young or insane. Allah (SWT) stated that: "Of their goods take alms so that thou mightiest purify and sanctify them…" (Al-Qur'an, 9:103)

Imam Ibn Hazim said that every Muslim young or old sane or insane needs to cleanse his or her wealth with Zakaat because of generality of the evidence. Anas bin Malik reported that the Messenger of Allah (saas) said: "Trade with the money of the orphan, lest it is eaten up by Zakaat." (At-Tabraani) In another Hadith Amru bin Shuaib related from his grandfather that the Messenger of Allah said:

"Whoever is entrusted with money of an orphan should trade with it and should not leave it sitting to be eaten up by charity." (Tirmidhi)

The point of reference in these reports is that the Messenger (saas) urged the trustee on the estate of people who due to age or other reasons cannot manage their own financial affairs, to invest it in a business that will yield a return and make it grow until they are in a position to do so themselves. For, if proper investment is not made with an orphans' inheritance, it will be depleted by charity, thus leaving the orphan with little or nothing.

The *Nisaab*

The Lawgiver, Allah has prescribed the minimum amount that is obligatory for Zakaat in different ranges of properties, and that minimum amount is known as *nisaab*. The reason for nisaab is to ensure that no one is forced to give Zakaat out of what he or she does not have, and that no wealth goes without Zakaat. Nisaab is also an insurance against the tyranny of the state to tax the poor and or the neediest as is the case in many countries. Nisaab is a reference point for the average Muslim who is not sure whether he possesses the minimum wealth on which Zakaat is obligatory. The wealthy need not worry about the Nisaab. Zakaat is obligatory on their entire wealth and must be paid out at the end of financial year that they set for their Zakaat.

The *Nisaab* will not be valid unless it fulfills two conditions:

1) The amount that has reached Nisaab must be the excess or surplus known as *"faadil"* from one's essential needs such as food, clothing, housing, vehicles, tools and machinery that is used in business. The essentials for living are exempted from Zakaat.

Although what constitutes *nisaab* may change from one country to another, the amount that is needed for the basic needs of living in different countries is very similar, because the market place determines the prices, whether it is an official market or a non-official market. In the poorest countries people do without or live below the poverty standard, and that is why many go hungry or without basic essentials.

However, we must realize that Zakaat is an act of worship (*cba dah*) like Salaat. The element of intention (*niyyah*) is necessary, and we should not overly rely on state agencies to determine for us the requirements of our religious duty. The so called the "consumption basket" (that is poverty level as determined by the social security administration which are updated every fiscal year) may not be the same as what Islam considers minimum *nisaab*.

In the industrialized countries, the consumption basket may include items that are not necessarily essential, such as entertainment, extra clothing, variety of food, eating in restaurant or eating at home, owning more than one car as opposed to having three cars in the driveway, drinking water as opposed to juices, eating regular food or special "health" food. This is why I believe it is essential that we do not lose site of the fact that Zakaat is *ebadah* of wealth, like salaat and fasting. Non Muslims may consider all the things mentioned above as essentials while Muslims will not. Indeed, no Muslim in good standing will attempt to hide behind the label of consumption basket so as to evade Zakaat.

Nisaab eliminates the possibility of injustice or unfair treatment of the Zakaat payer. To suggest that if we do not follow the rules of International Monetary Fund or the arbitrary figures of social security administration or department of agriculture we will be doing injustice to the Zakaat payer is ludicrous.

2) Nisaab must mature, that is the money is not liable for Zakaat unless it has remained a full year in the possession of a person. This is the understanding of the majority of the scholars. Imam Abu Hanifah (raa) said: "What should be considered is the existence of nisaab at the beginning and the end of the Zakaat year set by the payer." It does not matter if the nisaab money increases or decreases during the calendar year, as we will explain later.

This condition does not include farm produce, for it is due on the day it is harvested. Allah (SWT) stated: "...But render the dues that are proper on the day that the harvest is gathered..." (Al-Qur'an, 6:141) According to Imam Al-Abadi, (raa) Zakaat money is of two kinds: one that by its nature can not be invested and Zakaat of this category is due on the day of harvest. This includes all the farm produce that is liable for Zakaat. The other is wealth that can be invested in the hope of a good return, like cash, gold or silver, because the opportunity is there that cash in one's hand can be invested for a good return. This includes currency investment, merchandise and livestock. Their Zakaat is not due until they have matured in one full year.

The proof of this condition is the Hadith related by Ibn Umar that the Messenger of Allah (saas) said: "He who acquires property is not liable for Zakaat on it till a year passes." According to Ibn Rushd (raa) this is the understanding of the majority of scholars, including the four rightly guided Khalifahs.

Zakaat of Salaries

The condition of yearly term maturity applies to the commodities on which the Lawgiver said Zakaat is due, and this includes silver, gold, modern paper currency and livestock. Paper currency is analogous to silver, therefore, it takes the case of silver. There is no Zakaat on salary, earned income from wage earners or professionals or independent contractors until such money matures in a full year. There is no such thing as paying your Zakaat on the day you receive your paycheck. What the wage earner must know is that he or she can purify that money with charity (sadaqah) anytime they cash the paycheck. Allah (SWT) states: "And in their wealth and possessions (was remembered) the right of the needy, he who asks and he who (for some reason) was prevented (from asking)." (Al-Qur'an, 51:19).

We can deduce from the concept of "yearly maturity" of wealth on which Zakaat is due as encouraging, among other things, saving on the part of the Zakaat payer, and enhances the chances for eradicating poverty, because if the poor receives his rightful share of Zakaat there will be the possibility that he can take Zakaat money and invest it and become a Zakaat payer instead of recipient. This possibility will be lost if he receives few Zakaat dollars every month because he or she will spend it and may remain poor for ever. To say that the wage earner just brings his check home and spends everything on necessitites and lives from check to check with no left over savings means the person is eligible for Zakaat himself.

Using farm produce as analogous to salary for Zakaat is a wrong analogy. As Imam Al-Abadi said, these are two different categories of money. $2,500.00 cash can be invested by the person and expect a good return whereas it will be difficult to invest a bushel of corn. It can be traded as a commodity, which is what it is. This is why we must know that analogies have rules that must be followed before it is applied. Certainly the jurists are unanimous that earned income, known as almal al-mustafadah, should either be added to existing money and wait until that amount reaches maturity and then give their Zakaat; or if there is no money on hand the time one possesses this money, he or she should wait one full year before assessing it for Zakaat.

Zakaat is one of the five pillars of Islam and a vital element in the religion of Islam. It is the twin sister of Salaat. In Al-Qur'an, Allah (SWT) stated: "So establish regular Prayer and give regular

Alms; and obey the Messenger; that you may receive mercy." *(Al-Qur'an, 24:56)* Also, "...Establish regular Prayer and give regular Alms, and loan to Allah a beautiful loan...." (Al-Qur'an, 73:20) "And they have been commanded no more than this: to worship Allah, offering Him sincere devotion, being true (in faith); to establish regular Prayer and to practice regular charity; and that is the religion right and straight." *(Al-Qur'an, 98:5)*

In a famous Hadith reported by Umar Bin Khattab (raa), the Messenger of Allah (saas) responded to Jibril (as) and said: "... Islam is to testify that there is no deity but Allah and Muhammad is the Messenger of Allah, to perform the prayer, to pay Zakaat, to observe fasting in Ramadan, and to make pilgrimage to the house of Allah if you are able to do so...." (Bukhari, Muslim)

There is consensus among Muslim scholars that it is mandatory on every believer who is financially able. Whoever knowingly denies this obligation, while he possesses the minimum amount, would be considered a disbeliever and a renegade from Islam. Whoever is stingy, or tries to cheat, is considered among the wrongdoers. Zakaat is mandatory on four categories of items.

1. **Farm produce** of seeds and fruits, such as wheat, barley, rice, dates, raisins, cocoa, pistachios, coffee, cashews. Allah (SWT) stated: "O you who believe, give of the good things which you have (honorably) earned, and of the fruits of the earth which We have produced for you..." (Al-Qur'an, 2:267) Also: "...But render the dues that are proper on the day that the harvest is gathered... " (Al-Qur'an, 6:141) Thus, these two verses and many others indicate that Zakaat is due on farm products that reach the minimum amount *(nisaab)*. No farm product is liable for Zakaat unless it is a product that is considered as food and can be stocked or saved naturally without refrigeration. If the produce is perishable fruit, such as grapes, there is no Zakaat. But if one sells them they will pay their Zakaat on the profit earned when it matures.

The *nisaab* is 612 kilos, which equals 1,346.40 lb. There is no Zakaat on produce that is less than this amount. If the farm produce or crops grow dependant on rainwater, or without any man's labor or irrigation, Zakaat due is one-tenth of the total. If it is grown by irrigation, then the Zakaat due is half of one-tenth of the total produce. There is no Zakaat on fruits like apples or oranges or vegetables which are perishable and need refrigeration for long storage, but they should be considered as any income if the profit earned from their sale reaches the amount of Zakaat, then Zakaat should be given.

2. **Cattle**, including camels, cows, sheep and goats, that freely graze and are raised for trade and production. For Zakaat to be obligatory, the number must reach the *nisaab*. The *nisaab* of camels is five, of cows 30, of sheep and goats, 40. By freely grazing is meant the animal goes out to feed without the owner buying or bringing it feed or hay. If it is not a grazing animal, there is no Zakaat in the stock by itself. The stock will, however, be considered as articles of trade, then will be assessed for Zakaat as articles of trade when the profit earned from their sale reaches the amount by itself or in combination with other articles of the trade.

3. **Merchandise and goods of trade and commerce.** This includes anything that is obtained for the business of buying and selling: land, animals, food provisions, fabric, cars, spare parts, etc. The inventory is evaluated annually and assessed for Zakaat, whether the value is the same as the amount spent on it, more, or less. The owners of grocery stores, like any other business, must evaluate every item and give their Zakaat. Simple bookkeeping of inventory, orders, cash on hand, and credits, that is non-delinquent loans, will give one a good picture of the zakaatable assets. But if one is unable to account for everything in the store or shop, he should assess it according to his ability until he is sure that his conscience is clear.

There is no Zakaat on what is within one's dwelling or property which includes food, drinks, furniture, houses, animals, cars, clothes and shoes. The only exception is gold and silver. There is no Zakaat on assets from rentals or lease, whether they are apartment units, taxi cabs, etc. That is, there is no Zakaat on the apartment units, buses or cars for rental like yellow cab companies or trucks for rental or equipments. But there is Zakaat on the proceeds or incomes from these rental assets if these assets reach the executable amount, either by themselves or in combination with other assets.

Business Activities

Many scholars are of the opinion that any business activity that brings any return to the entrepreneur or investor should be assessed for Zakaat. If the activity has a prescribed *nisaab*, such as gold, silver or paper currency, that *nisaab* is applied for Zakaat. But if the business has no declared *nisaab*, its *nisaab* is the nisaab of commerce, one reason being that most business activities are considered as commerce and because, in actual fact, it is not factitious business name, such as GM, Apple or GE that is taxed for Zakaat, it is the individual investor. We do not tax cooperations such IBM, Apple, GM or Rajihy Bank but the individual investors, share holders and owners of these corporations.

Indeed, there are enough rules in Zakaat books to cover all types of business activity, be it cash or risk investment. If the business activity is analogous to commerce, it should be assessed the same rate as commerce. To subject the business to a different Zakaat rate of 10%, which is the rate of farm products instead of its correct rate of 2.5%, the rate of commerce, is unfair and unjustified. Besides, there is no proof, even a weak one, to justify this unfair arbitrary taxation. The difference between 2.5% and 10% is huge. The Zakaat system is not like a state revenue collection, but Allah's *ebadah*. However, if a business person decides to give more than 2.5% after deducting all the expenses including depreciation, Allah (SWT) will accept it from him.

4. **Gold and silver**, whether used for commerce or jewelry. Allah (SWT) states: "...And there are those who bury gold and silver and spend it not in the way of Allah: announce unto them a most grievous penalty. On the day when heat will be produced out of that (wealth) in the fire of hell, and with it will be branded their foreheads, their flanks and their backs. This is the (treasure) which you buried for yourselves: taste you, then, the (treasures) you buried." (Al-Qur'an, 9:34–35). By hoarding is meant refusal to give it in the path of Allah, which includes Zakaat.

In a hadith reported by Abu Hurairah (raa), the Messenger of Allah (saas) said: "For the owner or possessor of gold and silver who does not fulfill its obligation, on the Day of Resurrection it will be cast into sheets of fire and be branded on his forehead, side and back. Whenever it cools it is to be repeated for him in a day whose length is the length of fifty thousand years, until the judgement is rendered among the people." (Muslim). By its obligation is meant assessing it for Zakaat. In another version: "No possessor of a treasure who does not give its Zakaat..."

Zakaat is mandatory in gold and silver, irrespective of its form: in coins, raw or nugget, jewelry for wearing, or for rent, because of the generality of evidence of Zakaat without any detail. In a report by Abdullah bin Amr bin 'Aas (raa), he related that a woman came to the Messenger of Allah with her daughter. On the daughter's wrist were two heavy gold bracelets. The Messenger asked her, "Do you pay Zakaat on this?" She replied, "No." The Messenger said: "Would it please you that Allah will encircle you with two bracelets of fire?" The reporter commented that she took them off and threw them down in front of the Messenger, and said: "They are for Allah and his Messenger." (Ahmed, Tirmidhi).

The Messenger's wife reported that: "The Messenger entered into my house and saw in my hand a huge ring made of silver, so he asked, What is this?' I replied, I made them to beautify myself for you, O Messenger of Allah.' He inquired, Do you give their Zakaat?' I said, No,' or Allah willing.' He said: It will suffice you in the hellfire.'" (Abu Dawuud).

Zakaat is due on gold when it reaches the amount of (nisaab), which is 20 Dinaar. According to a hadith, the Messenger said: "No Zakaat on you is due until it reaches 20 dinaar." (Abu Dawud) The Islamic dinaar (currency) is one mithqal, a unit of weight which weighs four and one quarter of a gram. Thus, the nisaab is 85 grams. This is equal to $30.00 US dollars.

Similarly, there is no Zakaat on silver until it reaches five oqiyah, because the Messenger said: "There is no Zakaat on less then five oqiyah." (Muslim/Bukhari) Oqiyah is equal to forty Islamic dirhams. The nisaab is 200 dirhams. One dirham is equivalent to 595 grams. The zakaatable amount in both the gold and silver is a quarter of a tenth only.

Paper Currency

There is Zakaat on modern paper currency because it is equivalent to silver. During the early days of Islam, silver and gold were the currency of exchange minted into dirham for silver and dinaar for gold. Silver, not gold, had a larger circulation. Thus many scholars are of opinion that silver should be the standard for the paper currencies of today because that is more advantageous to the Zakaat payer, as it raises the minimum nisaab whereas gold lowers it. Although both metals are no longer circulated, they are still considered as a security against ever fluctuating paper money.

Silver should be used as a standard to assess Zakaat annually, not paper currency, even if the currency is hard currency like the US dollar, Yen and Deutch Mark or Pound Sterling. Because these currencies are backed by political decisions that may not have anything to do with the economy, the value and strength of this paper money depends largely on all haram usury system of interest rates.

Thus, the Zakaat payer should look up in the local newspaper's financial or business section for the price of silver which is currently about $3.82 per ounce. The nisaab, then, is $596 \times .04 = 28.80$ ounces multiplied by $3.82 = 90.91$. therefore. The nisaab is about $100.00, as of December 17, 1991.

The nisaab should be based on the market value of the currency. If the money is hard currency, there will be no problem, but if the money is a non-marketable currency, like most currencies in the third world countries, the nisaab should be based on the black market, which realistically reflects the value of the currency on the money market. In any case, the silver rate should be used to assess the Zakaat.

If the *nisaab* is determined, the zakaatable amount is 2.5%, or .025 multiplied by the amount. For instance, if the zakaatable amount is $56,000.00 it will be $56,000 \times .025 = \$1,400.00$.

Zakaat is due on gold, silver, and or paper currency, whether it is cash in hand or credit in the hands of borrowers. Zakaat is due on debts or cost of merchandise or rental money. If the borrower is a wealthy person that you know will pay back the debt, the lender (that is Halal lending free of usury) should include that money in the assessment and give its Zakaat. However, one can delay Zakaat on a loan until he receives payment, then return its Zakaat for the past years that he was unable to assess for Zakaat. If the borrower is poor or is refusing to pay the debt, there will be no Zakaat on the money until the lender receives the money. Then he will assess it for Zakaat of one past due year, but there will be no Zakaat in the years before that.

There is no Zakaat on precious stones such as diamonds, or metals such uranium, regardless of their value. Gold and silver, of course are assessed for Zakaat. However, if a person possesses any of these stones or metals, he should give their Zakaat like any other articles of trade. If a person possesses diamonds or any other precious stones as an edge against inflation or for ornaments, there will no Zakaat on these.

How To Give Zakaat

Zakaat may be assessed and returned in two ways:

a) Make a record of all money earned, either daily or monthly, which has reached the *nisaab* and remains in the treasury. The Zakaat of that money would be due one year later on the same day the money was earned and reached nisaab. This means every month's income must be set aside and assessed for Zakaat and so will be the case for the rest of the months. For instance, the income of January, 1991 will be assessed for Zakaat in January, 1992, and the income of February, 1991 will be assessed for Zakaat in February 1992, etc. This method of assessing Zakaat is very difficult because it entails complete bookkeeping of daily or monthly earnings.

b) The best way is to set a day or a month, preferably Ramadan, for your annual Zakaat return calendar, say Ramadan 1st, 1412. One year later on the same day Ramadan, 1413, your Zakaat is due and payable. Whatever is in the savings is due for Zakaat, regardless of whether all the amount in the savings reaches a year or not. For instance: if you have $20,000.00 in the savings account on the 1st of Ramadan, 1412 and one year later by the 1st of Ramadan, 1413 there is $50,000.00, your Zakaat will be assessed for $50,000.00, that is: $50,000.00 × .025 = $1,250.00. If, on the other hand, by the 1st of Ramadan, 1413 the amount in the savings is $15,000.00, your Zakaat will be for the amount in the savings, that is: $15,000.00 × .025 = $375.00. This method is the best because it is easy to assess, meets one's obligation, and relieve one's conscience.

The Recipient of Zakaat

Knowing who qualifies as recipient of Zakaat is an important aspect of Zakaat collection in Islam. Fortunately, Allah (SWT) has been merciful to us in that He Himself spelled out the people eligible to receive Zakaat. In Surah Tawbah (chapter 9) He stated:

"Alms are for the poor and the needy, and those employed to administer (the funds); for those whose hearts have been (recently) reconciled (to truth); for those in bondage and in debt; in the cause of Allah; and for the wayfarer: (thus is it) ordained by Allah, and Allah is full of knowledge and wisdom." (Al-Qur'an, 9:60) In this verse Allah enumerated the people who deserve this divine welfare, and they are as follows:

The poor and the needy. These are individuals, and those under their care, who do not have enough to live on. By the poor and needy is meant the people whose income or salaries, or whatever material goods they have, fall short of the cost of living in a given environment and economy. The poor and the needy should be given what will suffice them and their families for one full year. The needy who want to get married and have no means should be given enough for this purpose, and so, too, the student who needs money for tuition, rent, food, and books. The working poor should be given supplementary Zakaat. But the wealthy, or any person with enough income to live on should not be given Zakaat, even if they ask for it. Instead, they should be warned and admonished for asking for what does not belong to them.

In a hadith reported by Abdullah bin Umar, the Messenger of Allah (saas) stated: "A man keeps on asking others for something till he comes on the day of Resurrection without any piece of flesh on his face." (Bukhari/Muslim). This hadith indicates a humiliating appearance before Allah (SWT) that awaits a person who asks illegally.

Some said: this hadith implies Allah will punish a person with the very limb, the face, that he used to impress on others to give him their money unlawfully.

In another hadith reported by Abu Hurairah, the Messenger of Allah said: "Whoever asks people for their money so as to get rich, he is asking for flames of fire. It is up to him to ask for more or less (he should beware)." (Muslim) This hadith indicates the severity of the punishment, the more one asks the more punishment, the less one asks the less the punishment.

In another hadith, reported by Hakeem bin Hizaam, he said: "I begged the Messenger of Allah and he gave me. I begged again, and he gave me. I begged again and he gave me." He then said: "This money is green and sweet; he who receives it from people with a cheerful heart, Allah will bless him in it; he who receives it, with an avaricious mind would not be blessed in it. He will be like the person who eats without being satisfied; and the upper hand is better than the lower hand" (Muslim)

This hadith gave an analogy between money and green, ripened fruit that people love to eat. Thus, it indicates that both are greatly loved but easily finished. For money that is easy come easy go, one must be careful about the punishment that awaits the illegal eater. If a person asks for Zakaat and there are no signs of wealth, and he does not know that he should not ask, or a person who is well and able, who can work, but does not; if these people do not know that it is not permissible for them to ask, it may be given anyway.

In a hadith reported by Ahmed, Abu Dawud, and Nasaee, two men came to the Messenger of Allah (saas) and asked for Zakaat. He looked at them closely and found them strong and able, he said, "If you want I will give you. But you should know that the wealthy or an able person who can work has no share in Zakaat" (Ahmad)

Those who administer the Zakaat department, assigning people for collecting, bookkeeping, making lists of people eligible for Zakaat, and a financial calendar. These people will receive Zakaat as compensation for their work, even if they are wealthy. This does not include a person who works as an agent for one or two wealthy people to take Zakaat for himself. They should donate their time for Zakaat disbursement and do it with honesty and truthfulness. If they can not, they should be paid or rewarded for their time. In a hadith related by Abu Musa Al-Ashiari (raa), the Messenger of Allah said: "A trustworthy Muslim executor is the one who executes completely what has been entrusted to him of Zakaat money in good faith." (Bukhari)

That is, he will give the Zakaat money to any of the eligible recipients of Zakaat. He should carry on the duty voluntarily, but if he can not distribute the money without being paid, the Zakaat payer should pay him for his work. The payment for the service of distributing Zakaat should not come out of Zakaat money.

The new converts to Islam whose hearts we want to harmonize into the fold of Islam, either because their faith is weak or we are afraid of them being harmed, should be given Zakaat to strengthen their Iman or until we no longer fear their harm.

The bonds person who has contracted with his master to buy himself out of bondage deserve Zakaat and should be given enough to pay off their debt to the master and be freed themselves; similarly, Muslim prisoners of war if their freedom is tied to monetary payment, deserve Zakaat sufficient enough to secure their release.

On the other hand, if a person accidently kills someone and has no means to pay off the blood money, he should be helped from Zakaat funds.

The people in debt are of two kinds:

(A) The guarantor, who takes the responsibility of someone else's debt so as to reconcile the two warring parties, in order to extinguish the fire of *fitnah* between them. If the person requests Zakaat money to pay off this debt he should be given so as to encourage him to continue in this noble cause.

In a hadith reported by Qubaysah Al-Hilaaly (raa), he said I was under debt *(hamaalah)* and I came to the Messenger (saas) and begged him to help me pay it off. The Messenger told him: "'Wait until we receive charity, so we will command that it be given to you.' However, the Messenger stated: 'O Qubaysah, begging is not permitted except for one of three catagories of people:

A man who has incurred debt (as guarantor to reconcile blood wit) for him begging is permissible till he pays that off, after which he must stop it; a man whose property has been destroyed by calamity which has smitten him, for him begging is permissible till he gets what will support life or will provide him reasonable subsistence, and a man who has been smitten by poverty, the genuineness of which should be confirmed by three knowledgeable members of his people; for him begging is permissible till he gets what will support him, or will provide him subsistence. Besides these three, Qubaysah, begging is forbidden for every other persons, and one who engages in such consumes that which is forbidden.'" (Muslim)

(B) Whoever incurs debt and has no money to pay it back will be given from Zakaat to help pay his debt, whether the amount is large or small; or his creditor should be paid directly on his behalf, so long as it is paid off.

Zakaat can be given in the path of Allah. By this is meant to finance a *Jihad* effort in the path of Allah, not for *Jihad* for other reasons. The fighter *(mujahid)* will be given as salary what will be enough for him. If he needs to buy arms or some other supplies related to the war effort, Zakaat money should be used provided the effort is to raise the banner of Islam.

The wayfarer. This is the traveller who in a strange land runs out of money. He or she deserves Zakaat, enough money to take him back to his country, even if he is wealthy and can find someone to loan him the money. On his part, he should take with him on his trip sufficient money, if he is wealthy, so that he will not need Zakaat. Zakaat money can not be used to pay off other obligations, such as giving Zakaat money to people you are obligated to take care of by law; or Zakaat money can not be used to pay for hotel and food expenses.

It is, however, permissible to give Zakaat to a wife or family member, provided it is not part of their daily living expense money, but is needed to pay off a debt for one's wife if she can not pay it. So is the case for one's parents if they can not pay their debt.

Zakaat money may be given to members of the family for their expenses if one is not obligated to take care of them financially. The wife can pay off a debt of her husband with Zakaat money, because he may be among the eight eligible recipients and she is not obligated to spend on him as he is on her.

The eight eligible recipients of Zakaat can't be denied their right to Zakkat without proof from AL-Quran or Sunnah. In a hadith reported by Ibn Masud, his wife Zaynab heard the Messenger of Allah order women to give Zakaat, so she asked the Messenger (saas): "'O Messenger of Allah, you commanded us to give Zakaat, and I have jewelry that I wanted to assess for Zakaat, but my husband Abdullah bin Masud claimed that his son deserves it more than anyone.' The Messenger replied: 'Your husband Ibn Masud is right. Your son deserves your charity more than anyone.'" In another hadith reported by Salman bin 'Aamir, he said the Messenger of Allah said: "Charity to the poor is only charity, but charity to the next of kin is charity and maintenance of relations (silah)." (Nisaee)

No loan should be written off as Zakaat because Zakaat is taken and given. Allah (SWT) said: "Of their goods take alms. ..." (Al-Qur'an, 9:103) And in a Hadith the Messenger has been reported as saying: "Allah has mandated on you Zakaat to be taken from the wealthy and to be given to the poor." Thus, writing off debt is not taken. For instance, If you loan a person money, you can not write off that loan as a Zakaat. However, it could be written off as sadaqah charity. Furthermore, loan, delinquent or not, is considered an absent money, therefore, it should not be transacted in Zakaat, for Zakaat is assessed only on cash in hand. Besides, debt money is valued less than cash in the hand, and using that money for alms is like exchanging good money for bad.

The assessor of alms should try to give his Zakaat to an eligible person, but if he makes a mistake and gives it to an ineligible person it is accepted. In a hadith related by Abu Hurairah, he said the Messenger said:

"A man expressed his intention to give charity, so he came with his charity and placed it in the hand of an adulteress. In the morning the people were talking and saying charity was given to an adulteress last night. The donor said: O Allah, to thee be the Praise—charity to an adulteress! He then again expressed his intention to give charity, so he went out with it and placed it in the hand of a rich person. In the morning the people were talking and saying charity was given to a rich person. The donor said, O Allah to You be the praise — charity to a rich man! He then expressed his intention to give charity, so he went out with his charity and placed it in the hand of a thief. In the morning the people were talking and saying charity to the thief. So the man said, O Allah to You be the praise (what a misfortune that charity han been given) to the adulteress, the rich and the thief! Then someone came to him and told him your charity has been accepted. As for the adulteress the charity might become the means whereby she might restrain from fornication. The rich man might perhaps learn a lesson and spend from what Allah has given him, and the thief might thereby restrain from committing theft. (Muslim/ Bukhari)

THE LESSER HAJJ ('UMRAH)

Among the virtuous acts recommended during Ramadan, is performance of 'Umrah, the lesser Hajj, for those Muslims who are capable physically and financially first to travel to the House of Allah (Ka'abah) in Makkah, and who can afford the expenses of air fare or bus fare and accommodations.

The case for this 'Umrah rests on the Hadith in which the Messenger of Allah (says) said: "Performing 'Umrah in the month of Ramadan equals performing Hajj" (Agreed Upon)

This hadith indicates the merits of 'Umrah in Ramadan. It does not specify whether 'Umrah is performed in the beginning of the month or in the last ten days of Ramadan.

There is a popular belief that this 'Umrah should be on the 27th of Ramadan, the Night of Power. This results in a traffic jam on that date in the grand Masjid, with thousands of visitors around the world wanting to make Umrah on that night. As I have explained in the section on the Night of Power, the recommended act on the Night of Power is not 'Umrah, it is Tahajjudd (nightly prayer). After all, no one is certain that the 27th is the Night of Power.

Indeed, for those who can afford it and may have made Hajj, 'Umrah in Makkah during Ramadan is a lifetime experience that no one should miss. Words cannot describe the exhilarating feeling of Iftar (fast-breaking, nightly prayer, and Taraweh) in the Holy Land with other pilgrims.

EPILOGUE

Praise be to Allah (SWT) for the blessings of faith and may His peace and blessing be upon the Seal of the Prophets, Muhammad, his family, and companions until the end of time. The believer should be cognizant of the fact that the month of Ramadan is nearing its end and its departure is imminent. Ramadan may be a witness for you or against you. Whoever is blessed to fill it with faith and good deeds should thank Allah for the honor and must be assured of the reward in the hereafter. For Allah (SWT) will never deny a soul her just and complete reward. Whoever fills it with unseeming acts should return to Allah with repentance, which Allah has promised to accept.

Allah (SWT) has mandated acts of worship at the end of Ramadan to assist us in our desire to express our love for Allah, to strengthen our faith and increase the weight of our good deeds. He mandated fast-breaking alms (Zakatul Fitr) and legislated glorification and exaltation of Allah, (Takbeer) on the eve of 'Eid beginning from sunset until the time of 'Eid. He (SWT) stated:

"He wants you to complete the prescribed period and to glorify Him in that He has guided you and perchance you shall be grateful." (Al-Qur'an, 2:187)

اللهُ أَكْبَرُ اللهُ أَكْبَرُ لاَ إِلَهَ اِلاَّ اللهُ وَاللهُ أَكْبَرُ اللهُ أَكْبَرُ وَ لِلّهِ الْحَمْدُ

اللهُ أَكْبَرُ كَبِيرًا وَالْحَمْدُ لِلّهِ كَثِيرًا وَ سُبْحَانَ اللهِ بُكْرَةً وَأَصِيلاً ۰ لاَ

إِلَهَ إِلاَّ اللهُ صَدَقَ وَعْدَهُ وَنَصَرَ عَبْدَهُ وَ أَعَزَّ جُنْدَهُ وَهَـزَمَ الْأَحْزَابَ

وَحْدَهُ ۰ لاَ إِلَهَ إِلاَّ اللهُ وَلاَ نَعْبُدُ إِلاَّ إِيَّاهُ مُخْلِصِينَ لَهُ الدِينَ وَلَـوْ

كَرِهَ الْكَافِرُونَ ۰

ص ١٥٤

اللّـهُمَّ صَلِّ عَلَى سَيِّدِنَا مُحَمَّدٍ وَعَلَى آلِ سَـيِّدِنَا مُحَمَّدٍ وَعَلَى

أَصْحَابِ سَيِّدِنَا مُحَمَّدٍ وَعَلَى أَنْصَارِ سَـيِّدِنَا مُحَمَّدٍ وَعَلَى أَزْوَاجِ

سَيِّدِنَا مُحَمَّدٍ وَعَلَى ذُرِّيَةِ سَيِّدِنَا مُحَمَّدٍ وَ سَلِّمْ تَسْلِيمًا كَثِيرًا ۰

Allahu Akbar Allahu Akbar laa ilaaha illallah, Wallahu akbar Alllahu akbar wa lillahil hamd.	Allah is The Greatest, Allah is the Greatest. There is no deity but Allah, praise be to Allah, Allah is Greatest.
Allaahu Akbar Kabeera wal hamidilillaahi Katheeran wa subhanallaahi bukratan wa aseela	The powerful and abundant praises are due to Allah, and Glory be to Allah early in the morning and in the evening.
Laa ilaaha illallaahu sadaqa wa'adahu wa nasara'abdahu wa a'azza jundahu wa hajamal ahzaaba wahdah	There is no deity but Allah one and only, He fulfilled His promise helped His servant, strengthened His forces, and alone routed out the clans.
Laa ilaaha illah walla na'abudu illa iyyaahu mukhliseena la huddeen walau karihal kuafiruun	There is no deity but Allah, Him alone we worship offering Him sincere devotion even if the disbeliever distates (it).
Allaahumma salli 'alaa sayyidinaa Muhammad wa'alaa aali sayyidinaa Muhammad wa'alaa ashaabi sayyidanaa Muhammad wa'alaa ansaari sayyidinaa Muhammad wa'alau ajwaaj sayyidinaa Muhammad wa'alaa dhuriyyati sayyidinaa Muhammad wa sallam tasleeman katheeraa.	O Allah, evoke Your blessings on Prophet Muhammad the family of Prophet Muhammad, the companions of Prophet Muhammad, the helpers of Prophet Muhammad, the wives of Prophet Muhammad, and the descendants of Prophet Muhammad, O Allah, do send abundant peace on the Prophet.

Men will say this Takbeer aloud in masajid, marketplaces, in homes, affirming Allah's glory and publicizing his mercy upon them. Women will express their *takbeer* in silent voices as they are commanded to conceal their voices in public. Allah (SWT) legislated 'Eid prayer; it culminates the remembrance of Allah (SWT). The Messenger of Allah (saas) commanded his followers—men and women—to this *'ebadah* and his commands must be answered by all, as Allah (SWT) said: "O ye who believe obey Allah, and obey the Messenger, and make not vain your deeds." *(Al Qur'an, 47:33)* He commanded women to leave their homes for *'Eid* whereas their prayer at home is more preferable and better.

In a hadith related by Umm 'Atiyah, she said the Messenger of Allah commanded us to leave for *'Eidul-Fitr* and *Al-Adha* prayers including mature, menstruating women and virgins. As for the menstruating woman, they should keep away from the place of worship but should participate in good deeds and Muslim prayers. "Umm 'Atiyah interrupted O Messenger of Allah some of us don't have the outer garment *(Jalbab)*!' He replied She may borrow it from her friends'" (Muslim and Bukhari).

It is recommended to eat few dates in odd numbers before leaving for *'Eidul-Fitr* prayers in accordance with the report from Anas Bin Malik (raa) who said: "The Messenger of Allah (saas) will not start on the day of *'Eidul- Fitr* until he eats some dates in odd numbers." (Ahmed and Bukhari) It is recommended to go the 'Eid site walking instead of riding unless the place is far or the person is unable to walk due to age or illness. Men should wear their best but should avoid silk and gold. Women should dress regularly in a decent manner avoiding flashy or sexy outfits and perfumes in their outing for *'Eid*. *'Eid* prayer should be observed in the most humble and devoted manner.

The believer should praise Allah often and pray for His mercy and should remember the ultimate gathering in the hereafter (Al-Maqamil 'Aazam). He should be cognizant of the fact that there is inequality and disparity among the ranks of the believer on 'Eid day in terms of appearance as there will be disparity in ranks among the believer in the Hereafter in terms of deeds. Allah (SWT) (stated: "See how We have bestowed more on some than on others but verily the Hereafter is more in rank and gradation and more in excellence." *(Al-Qur'an, 17:21)*

The believer should be jubilant that he or she is blessed to fast Ramadan and has been able to observe prayers, recitation of Al-Qur'an and giving of Zakaat. These acts are better for us than this world. Allah (SWT) says: "Say in the bounty of Allah and in His mercy in that let them rejoice that is better than the wealth they hoard." *(Al-Qur'an, 10:58)*.

Indeed, if the *'ebadah* of this Ramadan is finished and over with the 'Eid prayer, the *ebadah* of the believer will not finish until death. Allah (SWT) states: "O ye who believe, fear Allah as He should be feared, and die not except in a sate of Islam" *(Al-Qur'an, 3:102)*. Also, "And serve thy Lord until there come unto thee the Hour that is certain." *(Al-Qur'an, 15:99)*.

The Messenger of Allah said: "When the servant of Allah dies his deeds are cut off." (Muslim) So far as he or she is still living, the service is continuous and uninterrupted until the end of life. The end of Ramadan does not mean the end of fasting; there is the highly recommended fasting of six days in Shawwal, and three days fasting in every month, as well as fasting on Mondays and Thursdays. Fasting most of Shaban and Muharram is recommended as well. If Ramadan is over night prayers are not. Praise be to Allah, this remains a Sunnah of the Messenger (saas) every night of the year, for ever. In a hadith by Mughirah bin Shu'ubah (raa) he said: The Messenger of Allah (saas) has regularly prayed at night until his feet swell. He was asked why (this hardship)? He responded: "Why shouldn't I be a servant who expresses his gratitude this way." (Bukhari)

In another hadith related by Abdullah bin Salaam (raa) the Messenger said: "O people decimate (salaam) salutations among your ranks, feed those who need to be fed and maintain the family ties, and pray at night while people sleep you will enter paradise with peace." (Tirmidhi)

The Sunnah prayers (Rawatib), before or after five daily prayers are 17 raka'aat. Four before Zuhr (Noon prayer), and two after; two raka'aat after Maghrib (Evening prayer); two raka'aat after 'Isah (Night prayer) and two raka'aat before Fajr (Morning prayer). In a hadith related by Umm Habeebah (raa) she said: "I heard the Messenger of Allah (saas) said: "Every Muslim servant who observed twelve raka'aat of superogeratory prayers other than the obligatory, Allah (SWT) will build for him a house in the paradise." In another version "Whoever prayed twelve raka'aat, day and night, Allah (SWT) will build with them a house for him in the paradise." (Muslim)

Remember the rememberance of Allah after Salaat. Allah (SWT) states: "When ye pass (congregational) prayer celebrate Allah's praises standing, sitting down, or lying down on your sides..." (Al-Qur'an, 4:103) The Messenger sought forgiveness three times after salutations from Salaat. He prays:

اللّهُمّ أَنْتَ السّلاَمُ وَ مِنْكَ السّلامُ تَبَارَكْتَ يَا ذَالجَلالِ وَ الإِكْرَامِ

Allahumma antas Salaam wa
ninkas salaam tabarakta yaa
dhaljalaal wal ikraam.

O Allah, You are Peace and from You is Peace, You are blessed, O Possessor of Glory and honor.

He (saas) is reported as saying: "Whoever glorifies Allah (*Sub-haanallah*) at the end of every Salaat 33 times, and praises Allah (*Al hamdulilaah*) 33 times, and utters the word of Greatness (*Allahu Akbar*) 33 times, that is ninety nine; then complete it one hundred saying:

لاَ إِلَهَ إِلاَّ اللهُ وَحْدَهُ لاَ شَرِيكَ لَهُ ، لَهُ الْمُلْكُ وَ لَهُ الْحَمْدُ وَ هُوَ

عَلَى كُلِّ شَيْءٍ قَدِيرٌ

Laa ilaha illallah wahdahu laa sharika lahuu lahul Mulk wa lahul H'amd wa huwa'alaa kulli shay in qadeer.

There is no deity but Allah. He is one and has no partners, sovereignty and praise belong to Allah, He has full authority over everything.

His short comings will be forgiven even if it is as large as fume of the sea." (Muslim)

Dear reader, strive in the path of Allah and obey His Messenger's commands. Avoid tripping on His commands so as you will deserve a good life in this life and in the life after. Allah (SWT) stated: "Whoever works righteousness man or woman, and has faith verily to him will We give a new life, a life that is good and pure, and We will bestow on such their reward according to the best of their actions." (*Al-Qur'an, 16:97*)

اللَّهُمَّ ثَبِّتْنَا عَلَى الإِيمَانِ وَ الْعَمَلِ الصَّالِحِ وَ أَحْيِنَا حَيَاةً طَيِّبَةً وَ

أَلْحِقْنَا بِالصَّالِحِينَ وَ الْحَمْدُ لِلَّهِ رَبِّ الْعَلَمِينَ وَ صَلَّى اللهُ وَ سَلَّمَ

عَلَى نَبِيِّنَا مُحَمَّدٍ وَعَلَى آلِهِ وَ صَحْبِهِ أَجْمَعِينَ

Allaahummah thabbitnaa alal Ieeman wal amal as saalih wa ahyinaa hayaatan tayyibah wa alhiqnaa bis saaliheena, wal hamdulillahi rabbil aalameen, wa sallaahu wa sallim alaa nabiyyina Muhammad wa alaa aalihee wa sahbihee ajmaeen.

O Allah keep us firmly in faith and good deeds and bless us with a good life and good living and make us join the ranks of the righteous people and praise be to Allah the Lord of the worlds and may His blessings and peace be upon Muhammad, his family and companions, Aamin.

This humble work was completed on Thursday 18th of Rabi'ul Awwal 1412 AH, September 26, 1992 AD by His humble servant Tajuddin Bin Shu'aib. Praise be to Allah in the beginning and in the end.

BIBLIOGRAPHY

ARABIC SOURCES

Al-Qur'an Al Azeem, King Fahd bin Abdul Aziz Al-Saud Printing Press, Medina Al Mumawwarah, Saudi Arabia.

Al-Ahadeeth of the Messenger of Allah (saas), Including Al-Bukhari, Muslim, Tirmidhi, Nasae, Ahmed, Ibn Hibban, Abu Dawuud.

Imam Al-Hafiz Ahmed bin Ali Bin Hajar Al-Asqalaani, *Fathul Baree*, Darul Maarifah, Beirut, Lebanon.

Imam Yahya bin Sharafud Deen An-Nawawi, *Sharhun Nawawi*, Darul Kutub Al Elmiyah, Beirut, Lebanon.

Imam Muhmmad bin Ali Ash Shawkaani, *Naylul Awtaar*, Darul Jeel Beirut Lebanon.

Imam Al Hafiz Muhammad Al-Murikfuri, At Tirmidhi, Tuhfatul Ahwazi, Maktabatus Salafiyah, Medina, Saudi Arabia.

As-Sayyid Sabiq, *Fiqhus Sunnah*. Darul Kitaab Al-Arabi, Beirut, Lebanon 1973

Sheikh Muhammad Bin Salih Al-Uthaymeen, *Majalis Ramadan*, Washington, D. C.

Muhammad Bin Alawi Al-Maliki Al-Hasani, *Qul Hadhihee Sabeeli*, Darul Medinah.

Imam Fakhrud Deen Ar-Razee, *Tafseer Al-Fakhar Ar-Razee*, Darul Fikr Beirut.

Abu Abdullah Muhammad Bin Ahmed Al-Qurtubi, *Al-Jamiu li Ahkaamil Quran*. Darul Kutub Al-Lamiyah. Beirut, Lebanon.

Imam Abi Hamid Muhammad Bin Mahummad Al-Ghazalee, *Ihyaa Ulumud- Deen*, Mustafa Babi Al-Halabi, Cairo Egypt.

Imam Abdur Rahman Al-Hareri, *Kitaabul Fiqh Alal Mazaahibul-Arbaah*, Al-Maktabatul Kubraa, Cairo, Egypt, 1964.

Abul Hasan Ali Al-Hasani An-Nadwi, *Al-Arkanul-Arbaah*, Darul Qalam, Kuwait, 1974.

Dr. Shaaban M. Ismaeil, Min Ahkaamis Siyaam wa Asrarihi, Cairo Egypt, 1976.

Abdul 'Aleem Abdur Rahman As-Sa'ady, *Siyamuka Ayuhal Muslim*, Ramado Iraq 1985.

Abu Muhammad Abdul Malik bin Hishaam Al-Himyari. Seratu Ibn Hishaam, Cairo, Egypt 1955.

ENGLISH SOURCES

The Holy Qur'an, Translations: Abdullah Y. Ali, Amana Corporation, Brentwood, Maryland 20722.

Imamul Bukhari, *Sahihul Bukhari*, Arabic/English, translated by Dr. Muhammad Muhsin Khan, Medinah, Saudi Arabia.

Abdul Hamid Siddiqi, *Sahihul Muslim*, Sh. Muhammad Ashraf, Kashimiri Bazar, Lahore, Pakistan, 1976.

Tajuddin Bin Shu'aib, *The Prescribed Prayer Made Simple*, Daawah Enterprises Intl., Los Angeles, California, USA.

Muhammad Husein Haykal, *The Life of Muhammad*, Shorouk International, London, United Kingdom, 1983.

Ibn Ishaqs *Sirat Rasul Allah*, "The Life of Muhammad," translated by A. Guillaume, London, 1987.

David R. Smith, *Fasting: A Neglected Discipline* Fort Eashington, Pennsylvania, 9034. 1954.